BASICS OF SOCIOLOGY

Volume 1

Bikram Singh

INDIA • SINGAPORE • MALAYSIA

ISBN 979-8-89699-737-5

Dedicated To

OUR DAUGHTERS, PARENTS, ELDERS, AND WELL WISHERS FROM VILLAGE RAJGARH DISTT. RAMBAN

AND ALL THE HARDWORKING, INNNOCENT, HONEST, SPIRITUAL PEOPLE OF

JAMMU AND KASHMIR WHO HAVE CONTRIBUTED IMMENSELY TOWARDS THE NATION BUILDINGS

SPECIAL THANKS TO MY BELOVED PARENTS MY BROTHERS AND SISTERS AND MY ENTIRE FAMILY WHOSE ENDLESS LOVE UNWAVERING SUPPORT AND SACRIFICES HAVE BEEN THE FOUNDATION OF EVERYTHING I ACHIEVE I AM ALWAYS GRATEFULL TO ALMIGHTY GOD AND MY SPIRITUAL GURU FOR THEIR BLESSINGS AND GOOD WISHES

CONTENTS

PREFACE

DEAR STUDENTS

It gives me an immense pleasure to present a book "Basic of sociology Vol.I which is intended as a standard tent for students taking sociology one of the subjects in 11th and 12th standards. The book is also useful for students preparing for various professional examinations like UGC NET, JKSET, Social supervisors, state PSC and those readers who want to gain a sound understanding of the basic concepts of sociology. The motivation behind this work stems from the growing need to make sociological knowledge accessible and relevant to both students and general readers. I would welcome the advice and suggestions leading to the improvement off the book. My sincere thanks to all eminent authors and publishers whose work and text have been the source of guidance to me in presenting this look I also appreciate the help given by MY BOOK MENTOR SHIVALIKA KOTWAL at all stages of the task. I hope this book inspires readers to see the world through a sociological lens fostering a deeper appreciation for the diverse and interconnected nature of human life.

Thank you

Bikram singh

CHAPTER 1

INTRODUCTION OF SOCIOLOGY

- Origin of Sociology:- Sociology is derived from both Latin & Greek origns.

- socius- Latin word - Companion.

- Logy Greeks word - The study of

- DEFINITION of Sociology:- Sociology is defined as the scientific study OF society, including pattern of social relationship Social interactions & culture.

- The term sociology was first used by Frenchman Auguste Comte in 1830.

- As social Physics later converted into sociology Thus sociology is defined as the scientific study of society social relationships its institutions and culture

INSTITUTIONALIZATION OF SOCIOLOGY

- SOCIOLOGY:- was taught for the first time at the university of Kansas in 1890 by Frank Blackmar under the course title Elements of sociology

- The fist academic department of sociology was established in 1892 at the University of Chicago by Albion w. small, who in 1893 founded the American journal of Sociology

- The first European department of sociology was founded in 1895 at the university of Bordeaux by Emile DURKHEIM

- 1904 - UK- Dept. of sociology at london School of Economics & Political science.

- 1919 IN Germany University of Munich by max Weber

- International cooperation - began in 1893 when RENE worms founded the institute international de sociologie later changed into the international sociological Association

- 1905 American journal sociological association

- Nature of sociology:- The origin of sociology linked with society and its institutions and deeply linked nature with human society

Different interpretations are given by different thinkers

- August Comte:- sociology as the science of social phenomena subject to natural & invariable laws, the discovery of which is the object of investigation. Comte proposed sociology to be studied in two main part social statics & social dynamic

- Spencer:- organismic theory of analogy in which society is compared with human organisms

- Max weber sociology is defined as the:- Interpretative Understanding of social action with the aid of an ideal type of behaviour.

- Emile Durkheim:sociology is defined as the study of social facts

- Robert Bierstadt in his book The social order enlisted the following feature / characteristic of Sociology

- Sociology is an independent science:- it means sociology has its own field of study, boundary, has method, and own institution not treated and study as a branch of any other social sciences.

Sociology is a social science and not physical science

social science	Physical science
Studied man, his social behavior	physics chemistry Geology
Activities and social life	studied natural laws
linked to other social science	not interconnected to social sciences

like history political science, Anthropology

Sociology is a categorical and not a normative discipline

categorical:- Focus on what is not what Should be or ought to be.

Cant decide right or wrong

ethically neutral

Normative Proper norms

decision making decides right or wrong.

Sociology is a pure science & not an applied science

Pure science:- Aim- acquisition of knowledge No matter, the knowledge is useful or not

It has its own applied field.

Applied science utilisation of knowledge.

Sociology is relatively an Abstract science & not a Concrete science it mean Sociology is not interested in Concrete Manifestation of human events but only explains the current issues

Sociology is an generalizing and not a particularizing science it means sociology doesn't study each and every events that takes place in society

Sociology is a general science and not a pure social science sociology is not specialized in one subject events or conditions but it is general in nature because it takes into account the general social interactions and social institutions under study

SUBJECT MATTER OF SOCIOLOGY

The focus of sociology is on individual and society and patterned social relationships as per the founding fathers the subject matter of sociology is as follows

AUGUSTE COMTE…..social phenomena subject to natural and invariable laws and studies social statics and social dynamics

MAX WEBER…..VERSTEHN interpretative understanding of social action

EMILE DURKHEIM…..study of social facts which are external to the individual and have constraining force on individual

OTHER THAN THIS …

STUDY OF SOCIAL INSTITUTIONS …family marriage kinship culture and societal changes

Formation and change of society from ancient to modern

Change of human nature

Changing societies and changing influence of cultural rituals on individuals

SCOPE OF SOCIOLOGY

There are two schools regarding the scope of sociology

- THE SPECIALISTIC OR FORMALISTIC SCHOOL

- THE SYNTHETIC SCHOOL

FORMALISTIC SCHOOL …LED BY GERMAN SOCIOLOGIST George simmel vierkandt max weber small von wiese and Ferdinand tonnies

Main ideas

Sociology is a particular social science and has limited scope

Unadulterated and autonomous branch of social science

GEORGE SIMMEL..sociology is a pure and independent science and has a limited scope It confirms itself to the study of certain aspects of human relationships only

VIERKANDT …it studies the mental or psychic relationships which links men to one another in society

WEBER..to understand and interpret social behaviour

SMALL.limited field. von wiese and tonnies expressed more or less of the same opinion

SYNTHETIC SCHOOL ….sociology is a synthesis of social sciences; sociology is a general social science

Main preacher EMILE DURKHEIM GINSBERG SOROKIN AND HOBHOUSE

EMILE DURKEIM sociology has 3 fields of inquiry

Social morphology; social physiology and general sociology

MORRIS GINSBERG…the focus of sociology

Social morphology deals with quantity and quality of population

Social control.Formal and informal means

Social processes.Cooperation competition conflict division of labour assimilation

Social pathology.Poverty beggary unemployment murder rape drug addiction etc

EMERGENCE OF SOCIOLOGY

ENLIGHTENMENT PERIOD …is the period of 18th and 19th century which involves the construction of new framework of diversity of ideas about man society and nature simply

HAVING critical ideas and knowing the reason behind the primary values of society

SOCIAL THEORIST

….KARL MARX.Theory of class struggle, historical materialism and dialectical materialism

MAX WEBER. Understanding and interpreting social action and the impact of culture on behaviour

EMILE DURKHEIM.Theory of religion suicide and theory of solidarity

AUGUSTE COMTE.Law of 3 stages

INTELLECTUAL IDEAS ….ROUSSEAU.Social contract theory

MONTESQUIEU. separation of power

AUGUSTE COMTE positivism

SOCIAL DARWINISM. .SURVIVAL of FITTEST TO HUMAN SOCIETIES it was popularized by Herbert spencer who argue that societies evolve through a process of competition and adaptation

MATERIAL DEVELOPMENTS

..INDUSTRIALISATION URBANISATION WESTERNISATION AND RISE OF NEW MODES OF transport and communication

Social developments

French revolution brings radical change along with

LIBERTY EQUALITY AND FRATERNITY

Growth of democracy EXPANSION OF DEMOCRATIC INSTITUTION along with freedom of speech and expression

Decline of Traditional social structure means breakdown of feudal and jajmani system

Diagrammatic representation
Dark ages 14-15th century

Renaissance-14th to 17th century
Dawn of modernity & its limitations

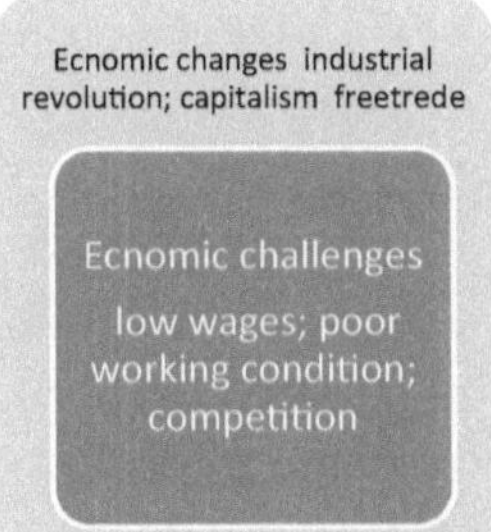

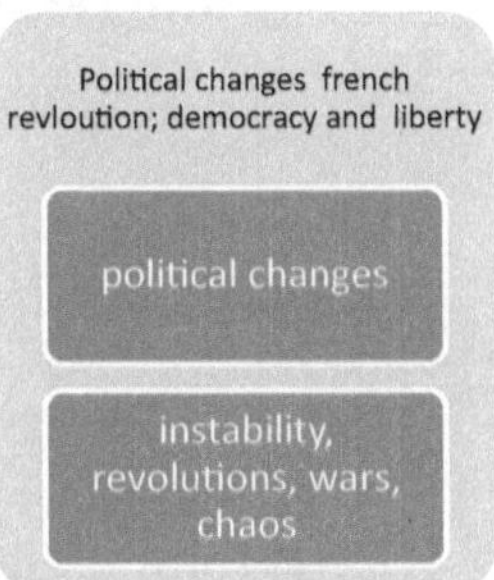

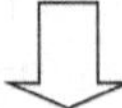

QUEST FOR THESE CHANGES LEADS TO THE EMERGENCE OF SOCIOLOGY

Society; Derived from latin word Socius which mean companionship / friendship.

A society is defined as a group of people who share a common culture, occupy a particular territorial area and feel themselves to constitute a unified and distinct entity In general society is the sum of interactions with the entire society.

According to maciver & page society is a web of social relationship

Feature/ characteristics of society

1. **Group of people:** without individuals no society forms individuals on the basis of society no society - no relationship, no social life

2. Social interaction i.e mutuals interaction among people

3. Likeliness: refers to similarities in terms of idea, value, culture, religions, outlooks

4. society rest on difference too: i.e biological difference between sexes personality traits, talents and attitude.

   Thus likeliness and difference go hand in hand

5. coperation & division of labour:

   CH cooley says, cooperation aries when men realizes that they have common interest

Division of labour leads to specialization both cooperation and division of labour leads to social solidarity

Interdepedance: All the social institution and social relationship are interdependent on each other like child depend on family for economic strength and family depends on children for emotional and old age support

Society is dynamic it means it changes across time and space

SOCIAL CONTROL both formal and informal means

CULTURE is the most essential facets of society as LINTON says THE SOCIAL HERITAGE OF MAN

FUNCTIONS OF SOCIETY

SUPPORT:- Support novel talents of Individuals

- women empowerment

- Collective Conscience

Socialization:- provider basic needs of its members; internalization of norms & Stabilization of adult personalities.

Transmission of Cultural norms & Values across generation.

- Social Control: regulates Social behavior of man

- Regulation of marriage all marriage practices and rituals depends on the ideas of all individuals

- Education society provides basic educational values like cooperation respect unity and honesty economic function all economic activities like production distribution and consumption of resources revolves around society

- Flow of information it play a vital role in spreading important information

- Preserving the heritage of knowledge benefits & Customs.

- Studying causes & consequences associated with social change

- Division of labor

Types of societies

- Hunting and gathering Societies:- Earliest form of society

- Hunting; gathering of edible plants fishing.

- Nomadic move Constantly

- Pastoral society:- Cattle rearing societies

- Agrarian society:- Agriculture

- Industrial societies:- Mechanization e.g invention of Steam engine in England and specialization of labour

- Information societies:- also known as digital societies based on ICT knowledge become more powerful. e-g U.S, Japan

Perspectives in society

- Functionalist perspective:- The proponents of functionlism are Herbert Spencer Durkheim, Parson etc.

- The functionalist perspective · Sees society as a Complex system whose parts work together to promote solidarity & Stability

Thus society is like living organisms in which each parts of the organisms contributes to its survival

Main Idea

Spencer Compared societies to living organisms and argued that as the body is composed of different. Organs & tissues and all there are interlinked and coordinated in a proper functioning of body it also further argued that in the same way a Society has a structure

→ Durkheim promoted that religion promotes the idea of Solidarity and unity within the groups.

→ Talcott parson for parsons, there exists a equilibrium & proper order within all the institutions of a Society. He compared the society to a motor Car

Thus society as a functionalist unit revolves around

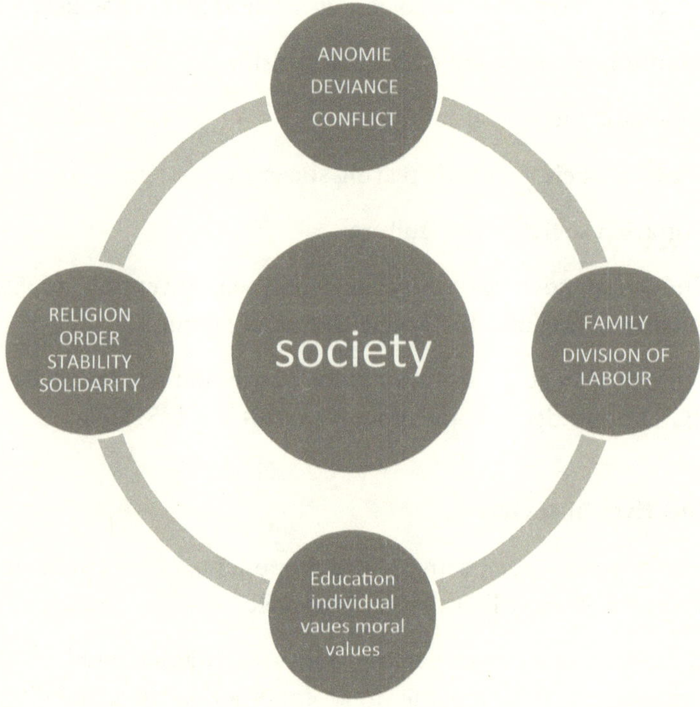

Criticism of Functionalism

It ignores the negative functions & too much relying on Functions

Functionalism exaggerates value consensus & social order

Functionalism ignores Class Conflict & Coercion.

It is conservative in nature. & ideological

CHAPTER 2

BASIC CONCEPTS IN SOCIOLOGY

SOCIAL GROUPS

It defined as a group of individuals who shares same cultures, customs, values, motives & common identity.

The great Greeks philosopher Aristotle said long back man is a social animal. As a individual in a society we belongs to various groups during lifetime.

Bogardus:- defines social groups as a no of persons two or more who have common objects of attention who are stimulating to each other who have common loyalty & participate in similar activities

Thus social groups are the foundational blocks of all society and necessary for the survival and continuance of people

Characteristics of social groups

Groups of people:- social groups consists of people, without people no groups

We Felling:- felling of oneness with the group members

COLLECTIVE INTEREST AND COMMON INTEREST

GROUP UNITY AND SOLIDARITY..members tied by a sense of unity

- SIMILAR BEHAVIOUR:- groups are formed between the like minded individual

- SIZE OF GROUP:- group size vary from region to region or communities to communities

- GROUP NORMS:- every group has certain norms which the members are supposed to follow norms in the form of customs traditions conventions and folkways

- GROUPS ARE DYNAMIC:- groups are not static They are subjected to changes . .old members die and new members are born

- STABILITY:- stability of groups based on individual ideology and group ideology

- INFLUENCE ON PERSONALITY:- social groups to some extent shapes the personality of their members and somehow depends on the charisma of leaders

CLASSIFICATION OF GROUPS

INGROUPS AND OUTGROUPS:- w G SUMNER IN HIS BOOK FOLKWAYS DIFFERENTIATES BETWEEN ingroup and outgroup

INGROUP …..we group

closed personal and informal group

OUTGROUP …they group

Represents formal and impersonal group

No signs of direct relations

PRIMARY GROUP AND SECONDARY GROUP

PRIMARY GROUPS it is the we group or informal social group characterized by face to face relationships concept of primary group given by C H COOLEY

SECONDARY GROUPS it is a special category group characterized by formal they relations and impersonal for eg political parties or large organisations like unicef

REFERENCE GROUPS the term was introduced by Muzaffer sheriff in his book AN OUTLINE OF SOCIAL PSYCHOLOGY 1948

ACCORDING to him the term reference group refers to a group that affects his behavior or we can say it is a group from which we are getting motivated and inspired to be a part

POINTS OF DIFFERENCE BETWEEN PRIMARY AND SECONDARY GROUP

PRIMARY GROUP	SECONDARY GROUP
Face to face relationship INFORMAL WE FEELING AND WE GROUPS	LACK IN INTIMACY & formal relationship IT REPRESENT OUTGROUPS
Smaller in size	Large in size
PERSONAL; CONTRACTUAL; NON SPECIALISED	Indirect IMPERSONAL specialized
Interest are not specific	MORE specific interest
Informal structure	FormaL structure

SOCIAL CONTROL refers to the control of society over the individual E A ROSS was the first American sociologist to give the concept of social control in his book SOCIAL CONTROL

ACCORDING TO HIM social control refers to the system of devices whereby society brings its members into conformity with the accepted standards of behaviour

PURPOSE OF SOCIAL CONTROL . .order;

- Stability;

- welfare;

- continuity conformity and

- solidarity

TYPES OF SOCIAL CONTROL

FORMAL ....IT INCLUDES LEGISLATION, MILITARY FORCE,, LAWS RULES REGULATIONS AND ACTS

INFORMAL ....FOLKWAYS, MORES,,, RELIGION MORALITY, VALUES,,, FAMILY and SOCIETY

AGENCIES OF SOCIAL CONTROL

LAWS ....official rule of a country or a set of rules by the government for all members of society to obey and follow e.g SC/ST PREVENTION ACT 1989,,DOMESTIC VIOLENCE ACT 2005;;RIGHT TO INFORMATION ACT

EDUCATION education is the most powerful weapons of social control it helps to identify right or wrong and increases the horizon of human intellect

CONTROL BY ICT it includes radio movies print media social media that issues warning and spread awareness

CONTROL BY FORCE eg military and police to maintain order and stability

CUSTOMS are the socially accredited ways of acting eg way of dressing eating speaking working etc

FOLKWAYS AND MORES folkways refers to the ways of people or the repetitive action of people

When folkways acts as the regulators of behavior then they becomes mores eg not to steal; always speak the truth stability

MORALITY refers to the conception of goodness or evil

SANCTIONS refers to the rewards or punishment used to establish social control

Status & role

Status is defined as position of individual in a society & role in the behavioral aspect of status.

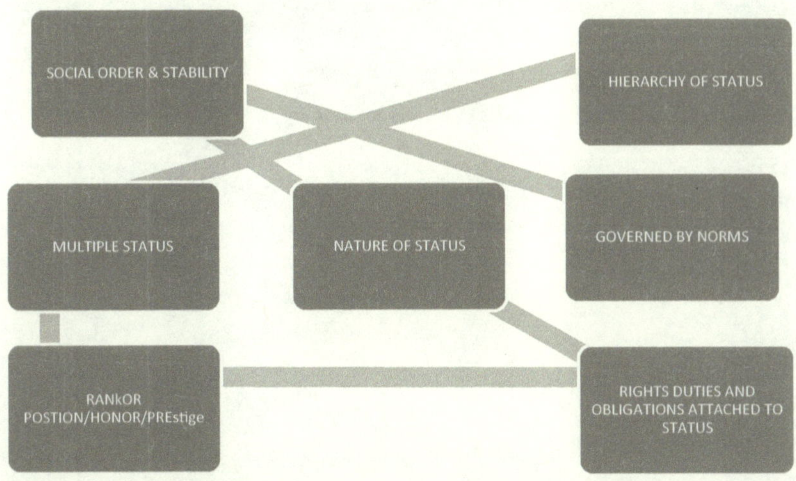

TYPES OF STATUS

Ascribed status:-status aligned at birth or on other basis like gender, race, family background

Achieved status:- social position that an individual acquires through their own efforts abilities & strength

ROLE:- is the behavioural aspect of status.

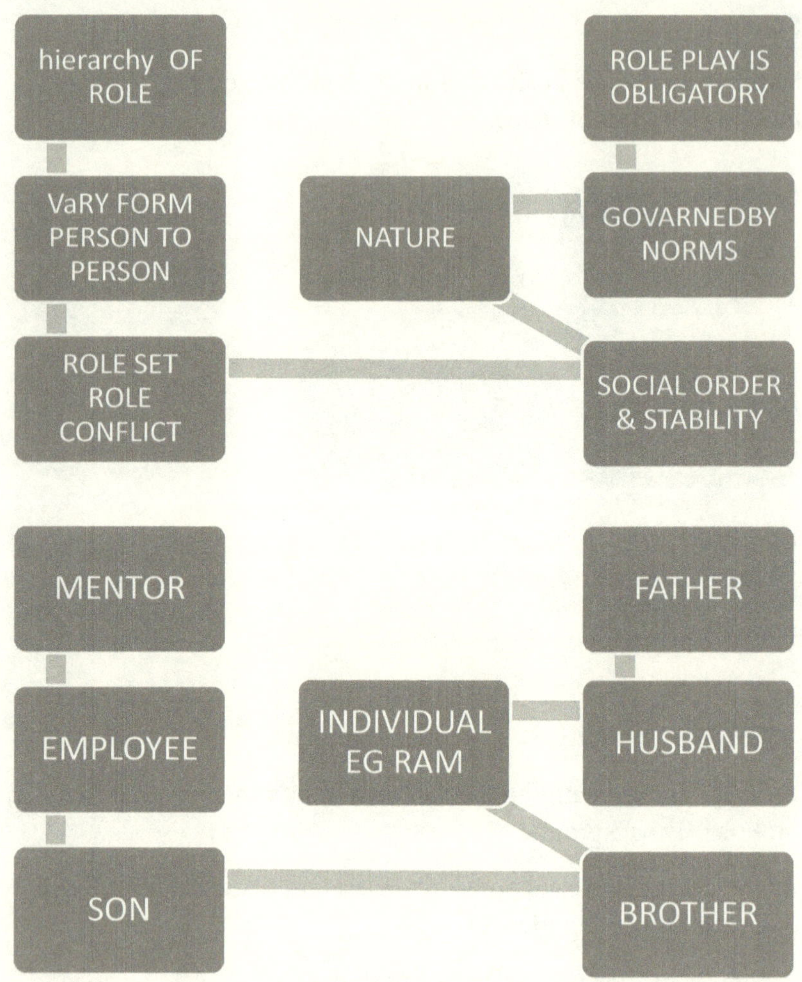

ROLE CONFLICT:-conflict experienced by the individual among different roles at two levels

(1) Within his own body of roles

(2) Between his own roles & those of other actors.

SOCIAL STRATIFICATION

Categorization and differentiation of people into groups on the basis of caste, class, ethnicity income, race gender, occupation etc is called social stratification. Or it a process of interaction of differentiation whereby some people come to rank higher than others.

MM TUMIN:- Arrangement of any social group or society into a hierarchy of position that are unequal with regard to power, property, social evaluation & psychic gratification

FEATURES/ CHARACTERISTICS

It is social: it means it exits in all societies & governed by social norms. & sanctions & ultimately connected with other system of society such as political, family, religious, economic education & other institutions.

It is ancient:- it exists since time immemorial

According to researcher; historians & others social stratification exists in even hunting & wandering society.

In hindu society

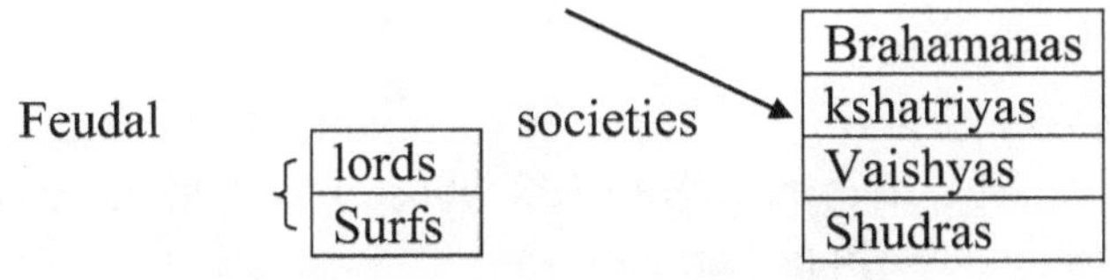

It is consequential:- Stratification has its own consequences. In terms of life chances & life style.

LIFE CHANCES:- refers to things such as infant mortality, longevity, physical & mental illness, divorce, separation etc.

LIFE STYLE INCLUDES:- mode of housing, clothing, residence education & modern & luxury lifestyle.

Determinants of social stratification

Determinants of social stratification

Caste

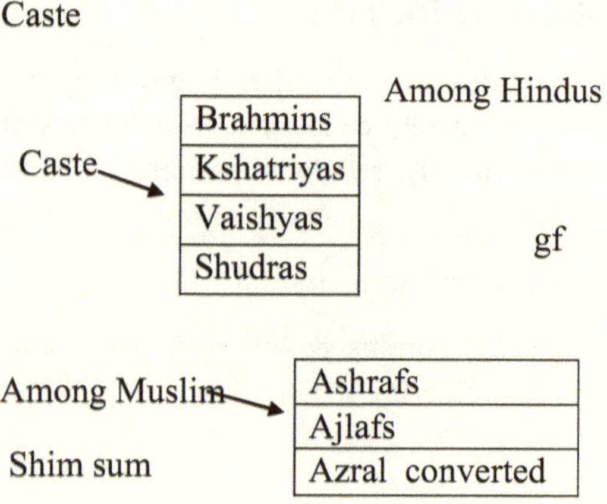

CLASS stratification is a form of social stratification in which a society is separated into GROUPS whose members have different access to recourse & power.

FACTORS:- wealth, income, education, family, background, occupation ownership of land property & means of production.

KARL marX bourgeoisie-rich class

Proletariat -poor class

Modern & western society

Upper class

↓

Middle class

↓

Lower class

CHAPTER 3

SOCIAL INSTITUTIONS

Kinship:> Refers to a set of individuals recognized as relatives, either by virtue of a blood relationship or marriage relationship.

According to **Robin fox.** Kinship is the study of mating, gestation, parenthood socialization which are considered the basic tenants of life

Principals of kinship;

The women have the children.

The men have sexual relations with the women.

Men exercise control.

Primary kin don't mate with each other.

In brief kinship refers to the bond of blood or marriage which binds people together in groups is called kinships

KINSHIP

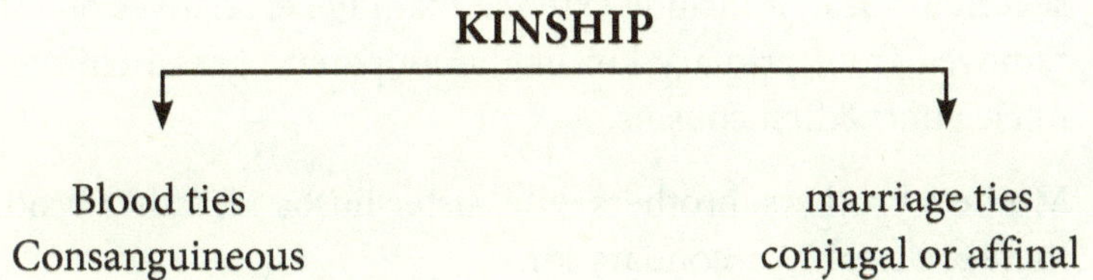

Blood ties   marriage ties
Consanguineous   conjugal or affinal

Team related to kinship

1. linage:> a group of consanguious descent group whose members trace themselves from a common known ancestor .

2. Decent refers to the social identity of the biological relationship that exist between the individual.

    There are rules of decent through which an individuals trace his decents.

3. Atrilineal descent: / agnatic/patrilineal kin ……. decent is traced through the fathers or male line.

4. matrilineal decent:> decent is traced through the female or mother. exclusively also known as uterine or matrilineal kin

5. Bilateral decants:> desecent is traced through both the lines the female &male the e.g is yako tribes of Nigeria also known as double descent

Type of kin

On the basis of nearness or distance kins are classified who the following

1. **primary kin:>** it includes immediate family members such as parents siblings & children's.

    There are 8 primary kin – Husband –wife, father, daughter, younger brother –elder brother, younger SISTER –elders sister &brother sister

2. **secondary kin**: it include extended family i.e. relatives one step removed from primary kin like grandparent, grand children's, uncle aunts &first cousins.

    Mothers brothers, brothers wife, sister husband, father brother there are total 33 secondary kins

3. **Tertiary kin:** it includes more distant relatives i.e. refers to the secondary kin of our primary kin total 151

Wife brothers son sister husbands brothers so on.

4. **Affinal kin:** > Relative by marriage includes mother in law, father in law sister in law, brother in laws etc.

5. Consanguinal kin:- blood relatives i.e. any family members related by blood like parents siblings, cousins & ancestors.

6. Fictive kin/ chosen family …. these are the individuals/ people who are not related by blood a marriage but all considered family due to close personal bonds like close family friends or godparents.

Lineal kin/ direct lineage …… it includes ancestors & grandparents, great grandparents and descendants like children & grandchildren

Kinship Usages.

Kinship usages refers to the ruler of kinship in understanding kinship system or it refers to the norms, customs, values, & practices related to kinship relationship in a society

Following are the kinship usuages

Rule of Avoidance:- it means kins of opposite sex avoid each other & it exists in almost every society which prescribe certain rules for men & women to maintain certain amount of modesty in dress & speech.

For-e.g. in Indian society father in law should avoid daughter in law or. GUNGHAT SYSTEM among DOGRAS AND HIGH CASTES

JoKING relationship:- in this type individual or groups is allowed to IMITATE OR mocks the other without any offence or friendly relations between opposite sex .

For e.g. relationship between grandson & grandfather or relationship between man & his sister in law;

Wife & her brother in law

Teknonymy:- it is most prevalent in Indian society i.e. a kin is not referred to directly but is referred to through. Another kin.

E.g. wife don't utter the name of husband. And his inlaws

Sonu ka papa sweety ke dada

Avunculate: it is a special relationship that exist between man and his mother brother MAMA this type is more prevalent in matriarchal societies.

Amitate: present in patriarchal societies in which fathers sister play a dominant role.(BUA)

COUVADE – it exist in mostly tribal societies & involves only husband &wife

Couvade a is cultural phenomenon in which a man typically the father, experience symptoms of pregnancy, childbirth or postpartum condition similes to those of his pregnant partner e.g. south American tribe

It reflects the deep emotional connection between parents & the significance placed on fatherhood in various societies.

RELIGION

Religions:- ReliGION is a part of human society since time immemorial it is a universal phenomenon & different scholars give different explanation there is no proper definition of religion.

According to MarXIST religion is an illusion which eases the pain produced by exploitation and oppression it makes the life Bearable & dilutes demand for change.

Feminist:- religion is a product of patriarchy

a product of dominance & oppression

According to James Frazer in his book

Golden bough considered religion a belief in power superior to man which are believed to direct and control the course of nature & of human life.

COMPONENTS OF RELIGION

1. Mans adjustment with the supernatural forces. Worship is the essence of religion

2. Social change:- rise of new religion new sects & new ideology.

3. Supplements empirical knowledge:ACCORDING TO

   Einstein:- science without religion is lame religion without science is blind

4. METHOD OF SALVATION in every religion there are prescribed methods of salvation to free from the clutches of rebirth cycle

   For eg in Hinduism methods of salvation are bhakti marg, karma marga and in buddhism the famous 8 fold path

5. SACRED AND PROFANE in every religion, sects and denomination certain things are identified as sacred and have religious significance

For eg neem tree and cow is sacred in hindu culture and pig is considered profane among muslims

FUNCTIONS OF RELIGION

SOCIAL SOLIDARITY UNITY PEACE ORDER AND STABILITY

SPIRITUAL AND MENTAL PEACE IN A MATERIALISTIC AND CHAOTIC WORLD

SOCIAL CONTROL THROUGH RELIGION NORMS VALUES CUSTOMS BELIEFS

SOCIAL WELFARE THROUIGH CHARITIES AND TRUSTS EG RAMAKRISHNA MISSION, SOCIETY OF JESUS

Provides recreation

Bhajans, fairs and festivals

Promotes tourism, revenue generation, employment,

Education:- role & functions.

The terms education is derived from the Latin educare which initially literally means to bring up in 1960-us president Lyndon Johnson said that the answers to all our national problems comes down to a single world education.

Definition:- according to durkheim educations is defined as the socialization of the younger generation a continuous efforts to impose on the child ways of seeing feeling & acting.

Function:

1. SOCIALISATION - transmission of values stabilsation OF adult personalities teaching honesty mutualism Fair values and integrity.

2. transmission of knowledge & skills seek practical life experience instrument of livelihood.

3. Personal Development

    o   Foster personal development & growth

    o   self confidence building

Self worth

*   encourages critical thinking & problems solving abilities

*   Economic development;

- Economic growth prosperity better lifestyle & chances

- Integration:- imparts values &

- foster democracy

- imparts moral values

- promotes integrity and brotherhood

- Promotion: health & well being

- Promotes:- globalization & global awareness

Promotes social mobility

- Structural changes in caste -system.

- Fights orthodoxy promotes liberal values.

- Initiate social change & helps to foster capacity to welcome change.

Equality of opportunity

Moral agent:- in ARISTOTLE words we become just by performing just acts, temperate by performing temperate one, brave by performing brave ones

Economy:- system of production & change

Economy refers to the system through which goods & services are produced, distributed & consumed in a society or a change of goods & services & creation of wealth.

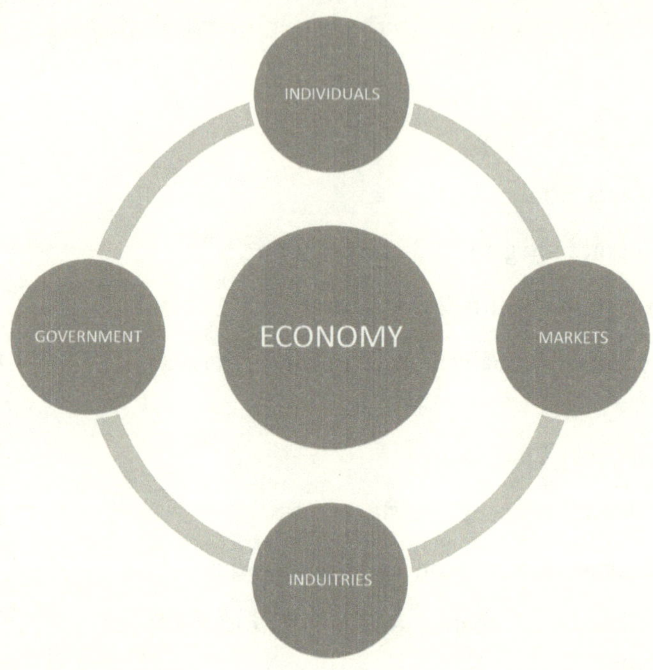

Types of economy

- Traditional economy:- based on customs, traditions, beliefs simply batter system or Jajmani system.

- Commands economy:- government or central authority makes all decisions about the production & distribution of goods & services.

- Mix ed economy:- mix of market economy & commands economy.

NATURE OF ECONOMY

Dynamic & evolving:- constantly changing to technological advancements & customers demands.

Interdependent & interconnected:- today the world is a global village e.g. economy performance of one country can effect others e.g. react Ukraine crisis & middle east crisis effects the global supply chain.

Resource allocation:- Nature of economy based on the allocation of resources to meet the needs & wants of society resources are limited.

Regulated & structured:- economy- central focus- growth & development.

Distribution and equity

Equal distribution & share to everyone social justice is the key concern

Sustainability:- balancing growth along with conservation of & preservation of resource for the future generation.

JAJMANI SYSTEM

Jajmans is a vedic term & yajman- means a brahmin/ persons/ priest/ landlord who conducted vedic fire sacrifice to appease god's

yajiman have a direct co-relation with the praja or the kamins

Kamins- persons who rendered services to yajmans.

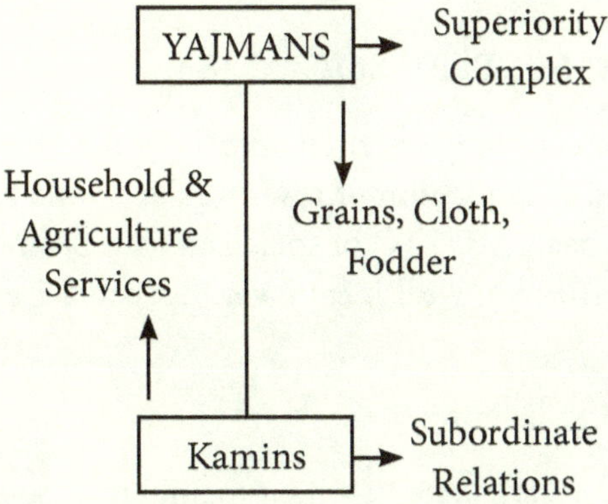

Thus jajmani system was a traditional economic & social arrangement found in rural India mostly among Hindus.

Key aspect/ features

Reciprocal services:- means specific castes provider specialized service to other in exchange for goods, produce (agri) etc.

E.g. barber, blacksmith. Provide service to the rich landLORDS

HEREDITARY IN nature:- it passed down from generation to generation within a familes.

JAJMAN relationship are EXclusive in NATURE MEANS providing services to particular individual.

Non-monetary transaction:- e.g. a barber receive some agricultural produce OR some clothes.

Social hierarchy it reinforced the caste hierarchy

High caste- more power & prestige

Lower caste- low power and dependent on higher caste for their livelihood.

EXPLOITATIVE -> some land lords exploits the lower caste & USE coercion / force to fulfills their vested and manipulative interest.

SOCIALISTIC SYSTEM/ SOCIALISM

It is a political or economy system where the production distribution exchange owned & regulation of resources are done by community as a whole. The basic MOTTO of socialism is to promote equality & reduce the disparities in wealth & power that can arise in capitalistic system

According to M.K. Gandhi

Socialism as a society is one in which members of society are equal none low, none high.

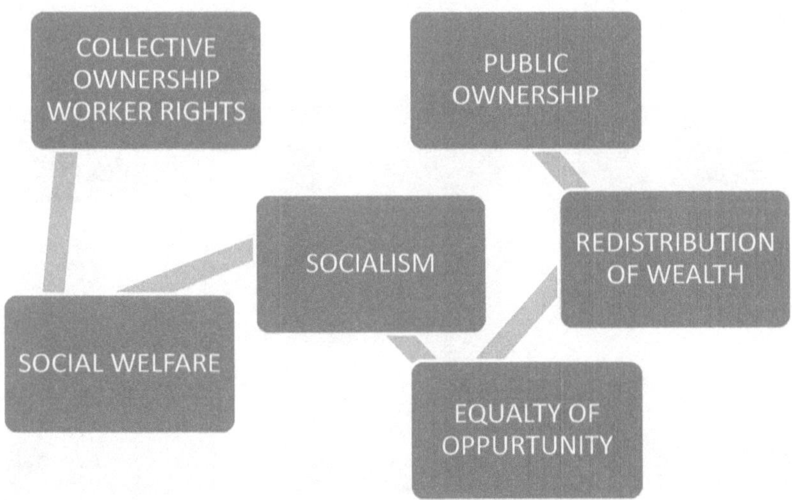

CAPITALISTIC SYSTEM /CAPITALISM

A economic & political system in which private individual or businesses own & control the means of production & operate for profit.

A capitalist system revolves around

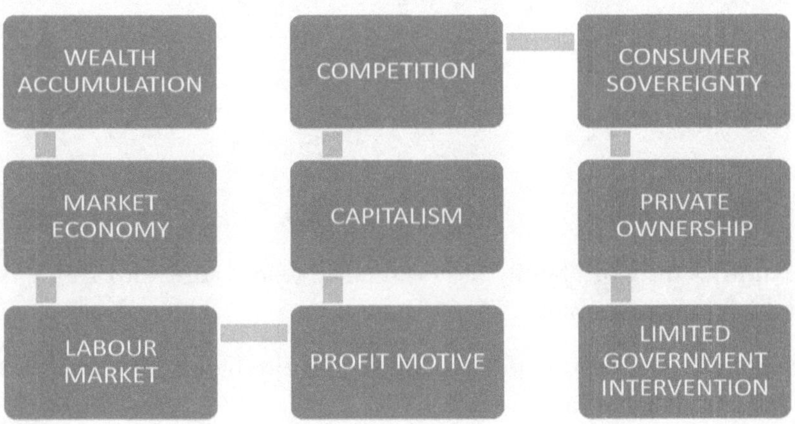

ADVANTAGES

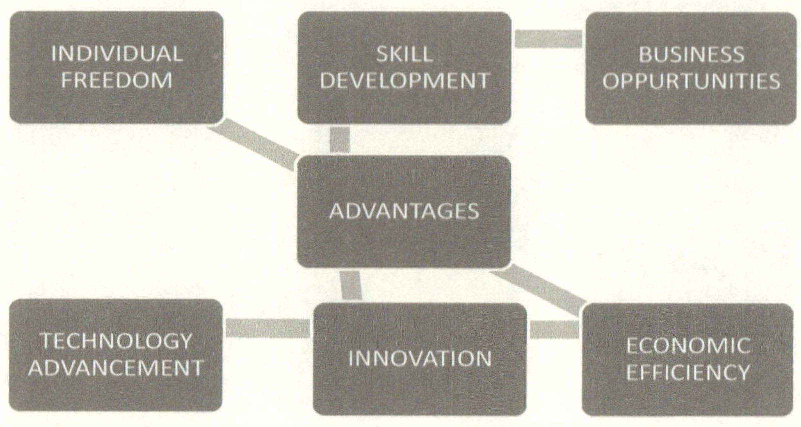

DISADVANTAGES

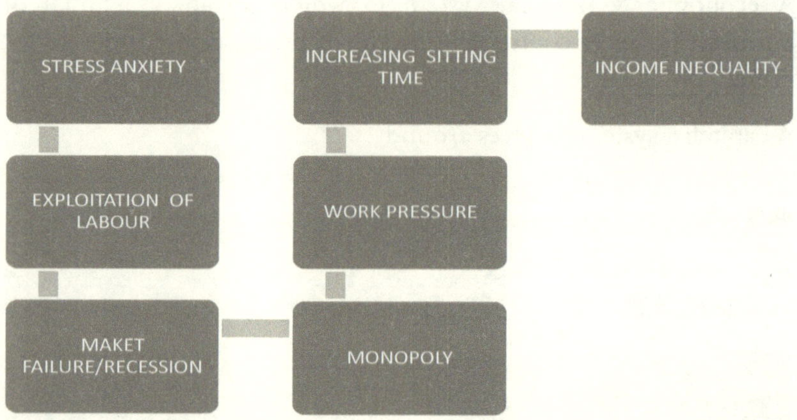

Family:- the word family has been taken from Latin word Famulus which mean a servant

Family is a group of person usually ties by blood marriage and cohabitation or adoption

in general it is a group of parents , children & siblings sharing a common residence & common kitchen.

- According to MacIver:- Family is a group defined by sex relationship sufficiently precise and enduring & to provided for the procreation & upbringing of children.

Features of family
FAMILY

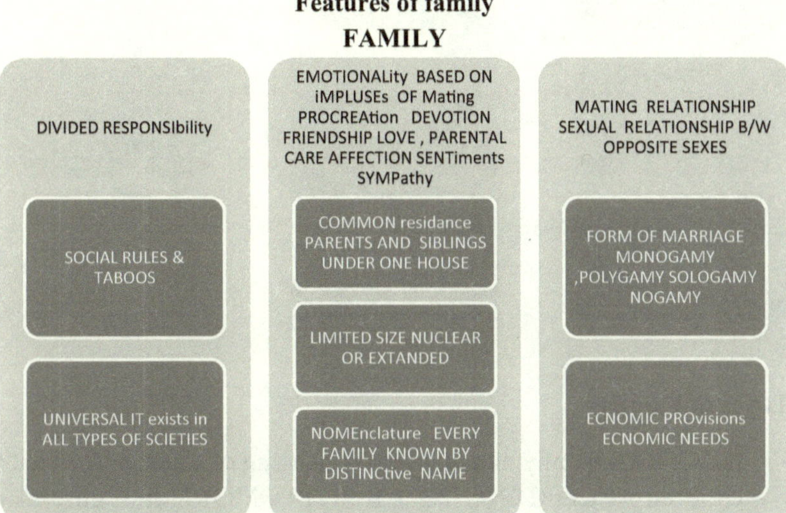

FUNCTION OF FAMILY

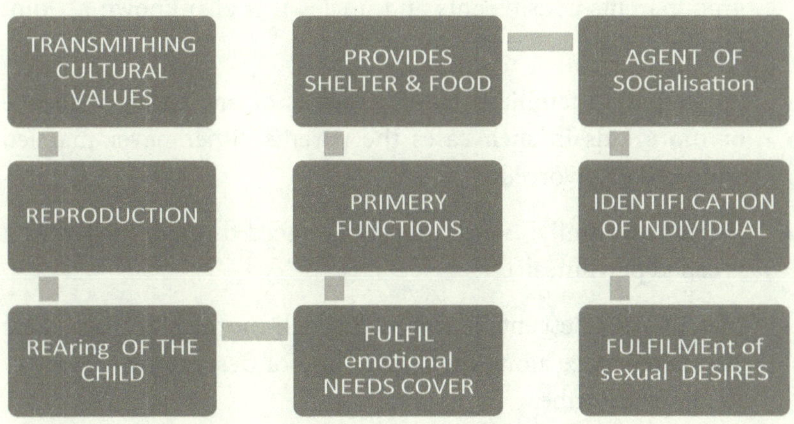

Primary function / basic function.

SECONDARY FUNCTIONS OF FAMILY

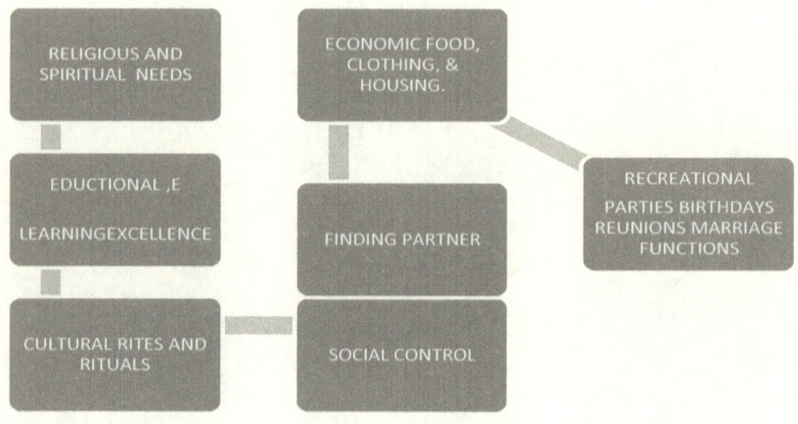

Types of Family

- NUCLEAR Family: Small group consisting of a husband, wife & children ACCORDING TO T B BOTTOMORE. It in universal in nature Modern Families are Nuclear families.

- Extended Family: Parents, Children & other relatives I e grandparents cousins ants and uncles it is also known as Joint family.

- Single parent families:- family consists of one parent with one or more kids in such cases the parents either never married widowed or divorced.

- Patrilineal Family:- when descent is traced through the father it is called patrilineal

- Matrilineal:- descants is traced through mothers & matrilineal also takes place along the female line of descent e.g. nayars of Kerala khasi tribe.

Marriage /matrimony/ Wedlock

Culturally & legally recognized union between opposite sexes.

According to Edward westermark :- marriage as the more as less durable connection between male & female lasting beyond the mere act of propagation till after the birth of offspring.

Malinowski says that marriage is a contract for the production and maintenance of children

FEATURES OF MARRIAGE

RESPECT TOWARDS PARTNER AND THEIR PARENTS

- COMMITMENT strong desire towards each other for a healthy and long lasting relations

- UNIVERSAL it means exists in every society and in every religion

- LONG LASTING marriage bond is knotted for the entire life even for after life

- SOCIAL APPROVAL without social aaproval marriage is not rewarded in societies it is governed according to societal norms

- RELIGIOUS CEREMONY marriage is considered a religious festival and is held according to religious ideology

- UNION OF MAN AND WOMEN marriage takes place between individuals of opposite sexes

OTHER FEATURES OF MARRIAGE

Mutual obligation:-COMPROMISE; FORGIVENESS; INTIMACY; REGULATED BY SOCIAL NORMS; SERVING ONE ANOTHER IN LOVE AND FULFILLING EACH OTHER DEEPEST NEEDS AND PRODUCTIVE ARGUMENTS

TYPES OF MARRAGE

Polygyny:- one man marriage more than one women at a given time

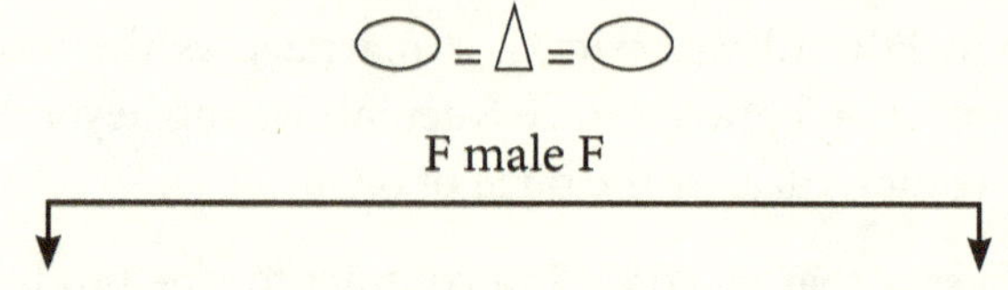

Sororal polygyny
Wives are invariably the sisters

non sororal
wives are not related as sisters

Polyandry:- one women marriage more than one men.

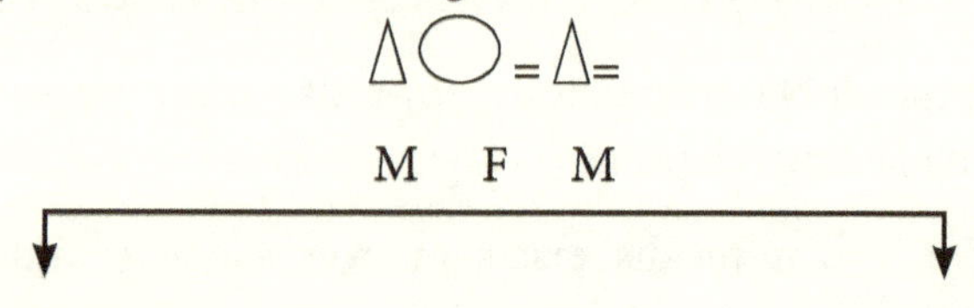

Fraternal polyandry
Several brothers' share
wife lending
The same wife
E.g. TODAS TRIBES

non-fraternal
wife sharing/

husbands are not related
as brother

MONOGAMY:- one men marries one women.

AUTOGAMY / SOLOGAMY:-first solo gamy marriage in India Gujarat by k SHAMA bindu

Act of marrying one self in public ceremony.

Other forms of marriage.

Cross cousin marriage:- when marriage takes place between ones mothers brothers daughter/ son with fathers sisters son / daughter.

Parallel cousin marriage:- when marriage takes place between the children of either two sisters or two brothers' e.g. among Muslims.

Levirate:/ devar vivaha when a women marries her husband brother after the death of her husband.

Sororate:/ Sali vivaha:- when a men marries his wife sister after the death of his wife or even when the wife is alive.

Anuluma & PRATILOMA	
hypergamy	hypogamy
men higher caste	men lower caste
women lower caste	women higher caste.

CHAPTER 4

DIMENSIONS OF CULTURE

Culture is defined as the collective beliefs, values, norms, customs, behavior and artifacts that characterize a group or a society

In general culture is the way of life

THUS CULTURE AS A WAY OF LIVING REVOLVES AROUND

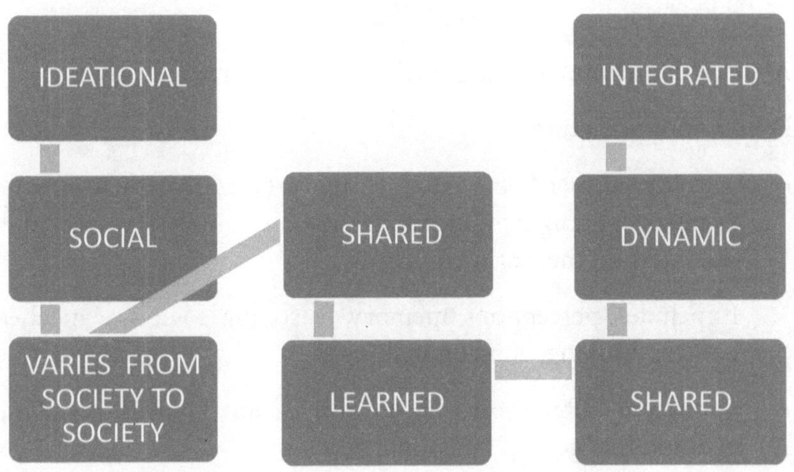

ELEMENTS OF CULTURE

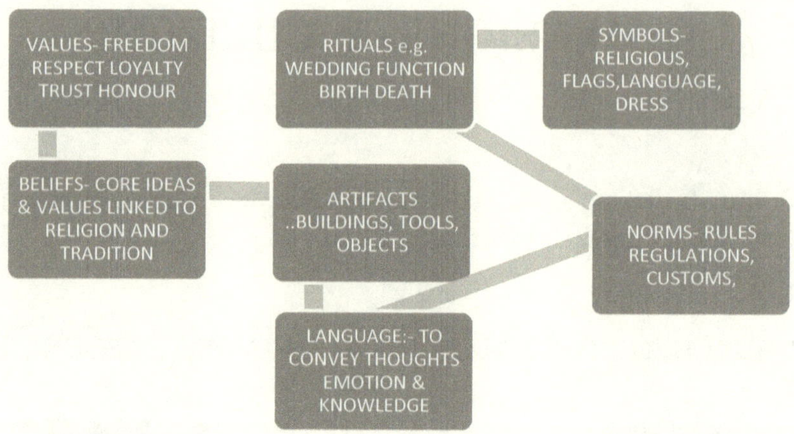

Artifact- It includes buildings tools object e.g. kirpan for sikh.

Dimensions of culture:

- Cognitive dimension:- refers to the process in which culture shapes over thought processes, perceptions & how we understand and interpret the world around us.

  It includes, perceptions, memory, reasoning, logic analytical & holistic thinking, decision making etc.

- Normative dimension:- it involves rules, norms, custom, tradition that govern individual behaviour.

  e.g. don't laugh at someone funeral.

  It includes folkways, morals, laws, taboos, values, sanctions, rules, & ideologies.

- Material dimensions:- refers to the physical objects, resources, & space that people use to define their culture. It includes the tangible aspects of culture.

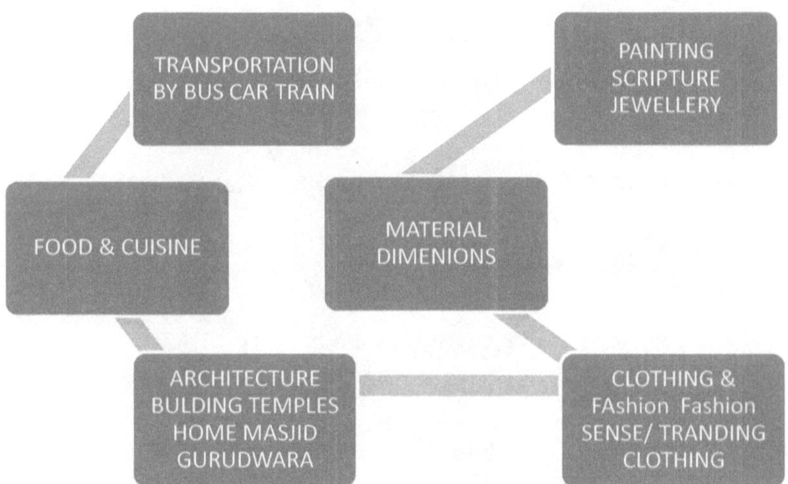

- Folkways:- a kind of social norms. The term was introduced by W.G sumner in a book" folkways published in 1906.

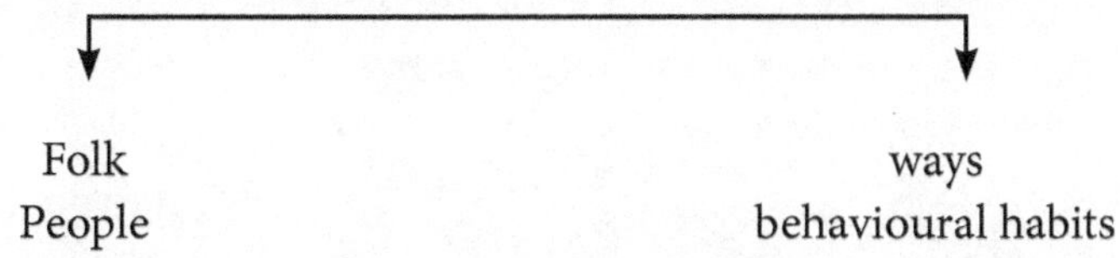

Folk	ways
People	behavioural habits

Thus folkways are defined as the traditional behaviors, customs & norms that are characteristics of a particular group, culture or society. Folkways are informal norms, not written but they are widely understood & followed within a community e.g.

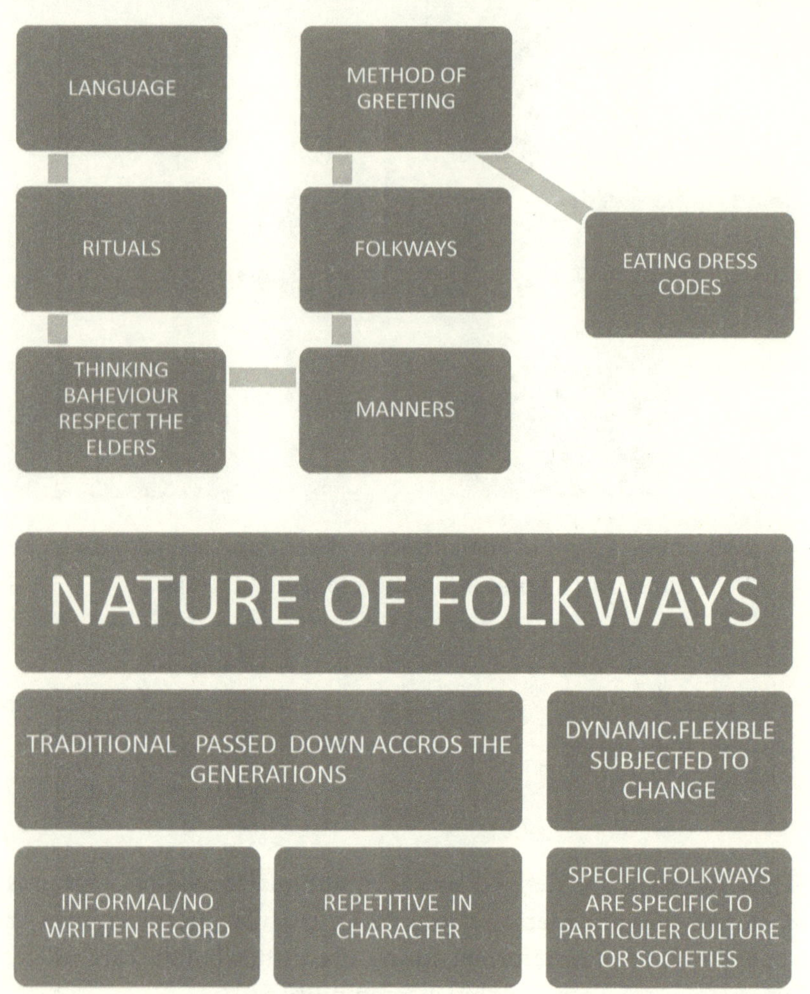

MORALS: it is also a form of norms that have significant moral significance with in a society.

It refers to the behaviour pattern which are not only accepted but are prescribed they are more formal then folkways MORES identifies individual with the groups and determine individual behaviour.

Mores have moral importance & closely related to a society ethical & moral beliefs.

Strong social sanctions-> violations leads to social disapproval, legal penalties.

CULTURE & HISTORICAL BASIS

Less flexible

mores are the guardian of social solidarity.

Norms:

Norms are the standards of group behaviour term given by M. sherif in book the psychology of social norms in 1936.

Norms are unwritten rules or standards that dictate behavior within a group or society.

They help regulate social interactions & maintains order by setting expectations for how people should act in various situations.

Features.

- Unwritten rules:- informal & not explicitly documented.

- Social expectations:- represent the collective expectations & standards for behavior within a society or groups

- Variability:- norms can differ greatly across culture, social groups, reflecting diverse values & practices

- Influence on behavior:- they guide individual actions & interactions, helping to ensure predictability & stability in social life.

- Change over time:- norms can evolve as society undergoes transition from ancient to modern.

Values

Values are the yardsticks for finding & measuring write & wrong, good versus bad, etc.

Values all fundamental beliefs or principals that guide behaviour & decision making in individual groups or societies.

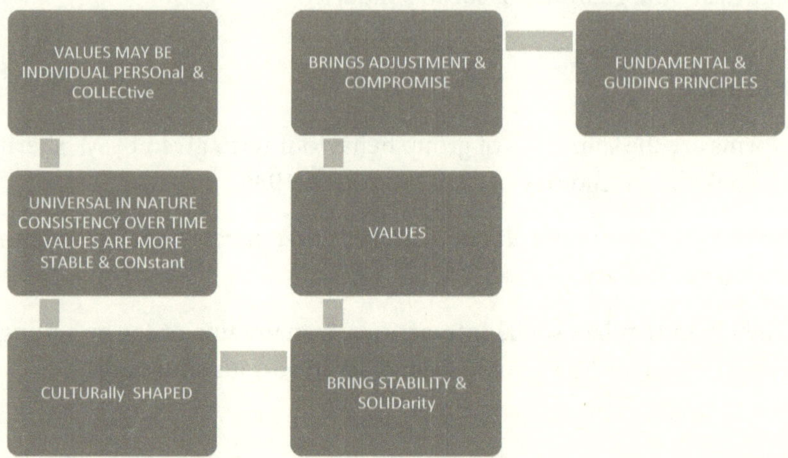

CONFLICT RESOLUTION - values help to solve conflict during crisis of conscience Value are hierarchically arranged e.g. integrity, honesty, truthness.

CUSTOMS:

Customs are traditional practices, ritual behaviour that are characteristic of a particular culture, community or society. They are often passed down through generations & play a significant role in maintaining cultural identity & social custom.

According to MacIver & page, the socially accredited ways of acting are the custom of society.

FEATURES:

Based on tradition:-customs are rooted in traditions & passed down from generation to generation.

- SOCIAL PHENOMENA:- customs are social in nature because it reflects the daily & routine action of individual

- Regional variations - customs varies from region to region reflecting local historical & cultural significance of regions.

- INFLUENCE ON DAILY LIFE:- customs impact a greater influence on daily life for e.g. greeting practices, clothing, fashion sense Manners, gratitude.

- SOCIAL SOLIDARITY - it promotes the solidarity via various means i.e. religious congregation, festivals, fairs

- REPETITIVE IN NATURE:- most of the customs involve particular actions, attire or symbols that carry symbolic meanings. For e.g. Diwali-festival of happiness.

CULTURAL ETHOS OF JAMMU & KASHMIR

Ethos: ancient Greek word meaning character, trust, credibility.

Ethos refers to the character, values & beliefs that define the culture or identity of a person, community

Or society. it encompasses the guiding principles & moral outlook that shape behaviours, attitudes & principles within a particular group or society.

Cultural ethos of J&K

Kashmiriyat:it is a centuries old indigenous secularism that promotes religious tolerance communal harmony and a deep sense of identity among the people of Kashmir. It lays stress on humanity, brotherhood and peaceful co- existence of diverse communities.

Religious pluralism

J & K is home to multiple religious communities like Islam, Hinduism, Buddhism, Sikhism etc.

Language

KASHMIRI

DOGRI

URDU

Literature: J & k has a rich literally tradition with poetry, pose & folklore.

Kalhana rajtarangini written in Sanskrit.

Lalded – A SHAVITE MYSTIC

Haba Khatoon: A-16th century Kashmiri Muslim poet & ascetic who was known as the nightangle of Kashmir.

Nund Rishi:- bringing Hindi & Islamic elements together in his poetry.

Art & Craft:-pashmina shawl, Kashmiri carpet, Papier-mâchie handicraft –featuring floral & geometric patterns.

Cuisine:- wazwan multi-course meal-Rogan josh, Yakhni & Gushtaba

DOGRA CUISINE Rajma chawal ambal nandru.

Festivals:- Eid, Muharram, Holy, diwali, loser.

Music & dance:- rouf & hafiza- Kashmir folk dance

Kod in Jammu. Chajja dance during lohri

SOCIALIZATION

Socialization is the process by which individuals learn & internalize the values, norms, customs & social skills corresponding to their culture or society. Socialization is a never ending & continues process.

Types of socialization

- Primary socialization:- it occurs during childhood or infancy stage of individual. It is the foundation stage which involves. Learning basic skills, language, culture norms & roles.

- Anticipatory socialization:- it involves preparing for future roles & responsibilities e.g. adopting behaviour & aptitude of a desired status or job.

- Developmental socialization/ secondary socialization:- it is a based on the achievements of primary socialization where individuals in lateral life encounter new environments, institutions & roles e.g. in government Jobs.

- Resocialization:- stripping away of old norms & adopting new ones. In a radically different social environment e.g. in military prisons.

Agencies of socialization:

- Family:- basic foundational stage basic values, beliefs, behaviours mother has a greater impact on Childs.

- School:- exposé individuals to diverse social interactions & help them understand the basic of equality, brotherhood, unity, compassion etc.

- Agemates/peers:- peer group also affect individual in all ways whether in streets, grounds, & during travelling.

Acquisitions of information, communication skills.

- Teachers:- art of learning skills, knowledge information & helps to maintain & stabilize personalities equality, uniformity, liberty, humanity, brotherhood.

- Media:- it shapes public perception, cultural norms & can influence behaviour & opinion on a wide range of values.

- Religious:- sense of community, shaping values, behaviour & morality.

- Workplace:- teaching individuals professional norms, ethics & behaviour expected in a particular workplace.

Government & legal system:- laws, rules, regulations & government polices & programs influence behavior by defining what is a rights or wrong or acceptable in society

CHAPTER 5

RESEARCH

RESEARCH

{Re-again, repetitive } search-to finds something. French word research-which means to search again.

Research is an attempt to know new things, facts, information, etc in a scientific manner.

According to kerlinger:- research is systematic, controlled, empirical, & critical investigation of hypothetical relations among natural phenomenon.

Features of a research:

(1) Empirical:- based on scientific experiments & true observations.

(2) Systematic:- follow proper order & sequential procedure.

(3) Objectives:- should be clearly defined, unbiased & objectives based on logic & findings.

(4) Generalizing:- the research should be general in nature & its findings available to large population.

(5) Welfare oriented:- toward the problem solving.

Objectivity:- based on facts & data & free from biases.

Validity:- degree of achieving the intended result or scores of a research.

Reliability:- to produce the same findings if the research is repeated.

Stages in the research

- Identification of problem:- this is the first step to study preliminary survey, case studies.

- Revivew the literature:- to study the existing literature regarding the problem its helps to understand the topic, identify the gaps & helps in formulating research hypotheses & objectives. Books, magazines, research journal.

Formation of research hypothesis:-

- Hypotheses:-tentative statement about the research problem which formulates a precise & definite relation between two or more variables. It serve as the guiding focus of investigation.

- Research desing:-it is the master plan how research is conducted. It briefly enplains the research method & methodology in conducting research.

Collecting data:- methods

Qualitative   QUANTITATIVE
Observation   survey, interviews.

Ethnography.

- Analyzing data:-it involves a number of closely related stages i.e. categorization of data & applying coding & tabulation and then drawing statistical conclusions.

- Interpreting results:- this stage determines whether the results align with the research problem i.e. support the problem or refute the hypothesis.

- Drawing conclusions:- based on the interpretation conclusions are made regarding the research problem.

- Report writing:- it is the final stage which involves writing up research finding in a formal report.

Importance of research:

(1) Advancement of knowledge:- research expands our understanding of the world, filling gaps in knowledge & providing new insights.

(2) Informed decision making:- evidence based information helps in proper decision making.

(3) Problem solving:- Research identifies, analyzes & providing solution to various society, scientific & technical problems.

(4) Critical thinking:- research requires critical thinking, which is the ability to think rationally, analyze information & make connections.

(5) Improving quality of life.

(6) Personal & protection growth.

(7) It brings social change.

(8) Research leads to policy formation.

(9) Preservation of History, cultural & artefacts

Global collaboration & promotes the innovation era.

Research methods:

Techniques or strategies used to collect analyze & interpret data in a structured & systematic way.

Two types

QUALITATIVE	QUANTITATIVE
Based on experiences, opinions idea & understanding concepts	Based on numerical & quantifiable data
Subjective in nature e.g. interviews, observations, focused group discussions case studies content analysis ethnography	Objective in nature e.g. surveys, questionnaires statistical analysis, longitudinal studies experiments close ended questions sampling
Validity & reliability is difficult to check	Easy to check
Options based on -open ended questions	Fixed response options

QUALITATIVE METHODS:

- Observation:- it is a qualitative methods of data collection in which data is collected systematically by watching & recording behavior, events or phenomena in a natural or controlled environment.

- According to P V YOUNG:- observation is a systematic viewing along with consideration of seen phenomenon.

It is method of watching & observing the various event related to research problem.

Types of observation

Structured & unstructured observation:

- Predefined set of criteria to systematically observe & record specific behaviour or event.

- Close ended questions.

Unstructured:

- no predefined plan

- open ended questions.

Participant, QUASI PARTICIPANT AND NON PARTICIPANT –.

- Participant:- the research become actively involved in the environment or group being studied.

- Non-participant:- the research keeps aloof & observes the subject as they act.

- Quasi-participant:- it is also based on principles of participant observation, but the degree of involvement is less. It combines participant & non-participant.

- Naturalistic observation:- observing participants in their natural environment without interfering with their behaviour. It is often used in psychology, animal behavior studies & anthropology.

- Controlled observation:- the researcher observes behavior in a controlled or laboratory setting where variables can be manipulated used in experimental psychology or behavioural science research.

Advantages:

(1) Data obtained in a natural setting without interference.

(2) Useful for exploratory research.

(3) It allows researcher to collect data in real time capturing events and provide more accuracy.

(4) It opens researcher mind's to new possibilities that might not have considered before.

(5) Researcher can collect authentic data and avoid any potential problems with self reported data.

Disadvantages:

(1) Time consuming.

(2) Researcher biasness

(3) Limited generaliziability

(4) Ethical issues - i.e. breach the privacy of subjects.

(1) Resource intensive.

(2) Validity & Reliability is difficult to achieve.

(3) Challenging to conduct study on a wider scale.

(4) Need of Skilled researcher.

INTERVIEW

Interview:- it is guided conversation between researcher and the respondent interview is a technique in which there is a one to one interaction between subjects and the researcher

IT is a qualitative method of data collection and takes place in various forms and types like face-face, telephonic and groups' interview.

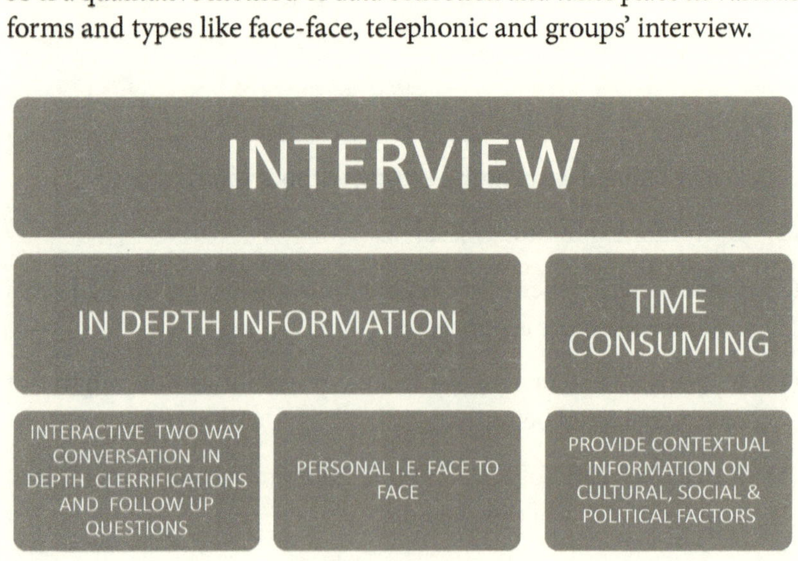

TYPES

- Structured interviews:- Follow A fixed format per-set questions in order close ending questions.

- Unstructured:- open ended question flexibility & greater freedom in the interview natural conversations

- SEMI -Structured interviews:- structured+ unstructured follow up questions & open ended questions.

- Group interviews (focus groups) it involves multiple participants who arrange in a facilitated discussions on specific topic.

- NARRATIVE interviews:- focus on participants personal stories, views, experiences and narratives

Advantage:

(1) In general interviews are more flexible.

(2) Cover Larger samples.

(3) Validity is confirmed.

(4) Response rate high.

(5) They overcome problems with literacy.

Disadvantage:

- costly affair

- Researcher/interviews bias, respondent basic problems of validity & reliability

- social bias in which respondent often make such answer which they think present their best image

- Limited respondent can be interviewed

- amount of information is also limited.

Language is also another barrier, individual accent, pronunciation; dialectics can also make the situation worse for researcher.

Interview schedule:- in a list containing a set of structured questions that have been prepared to serve as a guide for interviews, researcher and investigators in collection information or data about specific topic the schedule is filled by the researcher himself (interviewer).

Case study:- it is a complete and detailed account of a single social phenomenon in which in depth details of an event are studied. Or in depths examinations of particular individual, groups, organization or event to explore causes and effect.

They are widely used in business laws, medicinal, and social sciences.

QUANTITATIVE METHODS:

Questionnaire:- it is a quantitative method to collect data from respondents through a series of questions

It has per-set questions in a pre set order to gather information on opinion, behaviour, experience or other variables of interests

Questionnaires can be structured or unstructured depending on researcher needs.

Features of a good questionnaires

- Clarity avoid ambiguity or jargon terms

- easy to understand

- Relevance:- questions should be directly related to the research topic.

- Use of simple language & straightforward sentence structure.

- Complex questions should be avoided

- Objectivity:- unbiased, neutral questions.

- Structured responses:- close ended questions with precise options.

- Pilot test:- conduces pilot study before the actual questionnaire.

Advantage:

- Response rate is higher.

- Objectivity.

- Cost effectiveness.

- Time savings

- Longitudinal studies: questionnaires facilitates longitudinal Studies allowing researcher to track changes in attitude behaviour and opinions over extended periods,

Disadvantage:

- Limited information. In depth detail can't be extracted

- Data security & privacy concern e.g. online questions may raise concern about data security & privacy breaches.

- Respondent may be biased towards questions to project himself/ herself of morally or socially correct.

- Not applied to illiterate masses.

Response rate in cases of online & mail questionnaire is very low

Interpreting of questionnaire by the respondent quite pose a threat to the

Research topic.

Difficult to gain sensitive information because people are not ready to disclose.

SAMPLING

Sampling is a process of selection of a limited number of item from a large whole or universe of items or target. Population

Target population is that population which is choosen by the researcher for study

It is a quantitative method of data collection and it represents a representative set of data which stand for whole the population.

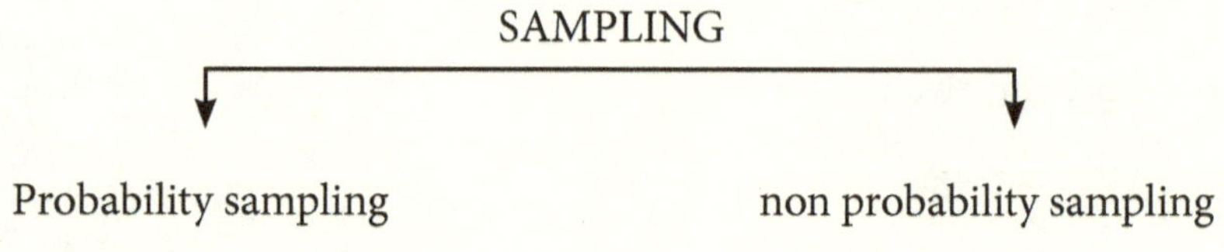

In this method every element in the sample population has equal change of being selected

it ensure equal representation as each item has equal change of being selected.

Types:

- lottery or simple random sampling:- every member of the population has equal chances of being chosen.

- It is the simplest form of sampling with highest degree of randomness and hence is a true probability sampling.

Systematic random sampling / interval:

Researcher selects every nth individual from a sample population.

- Stratified sampling:- sampling in which total population is divided into smaller groups or stratas to complete the sampling process. The strata is based on some common characteristics in the population data after stratas the researcher randomly select the sample proportionally.

- Cluster sampling:- the population is divided into clusters usually based on geography and a random selection of cluster is chosen then all individuals or a random sample within the selected cultures are studied.

- Non-probability sampling / non random sampling method / exploratory.

N.P.S is used when it is difficult or impossible to use a random selection it is more common in qualitative research or exploratory studies the findings may not be the true representative of entire population.

TYPES:

Convenience sampling / accidental sampling:

The sample is taken from a group that is easy to access for e.g. surveying people at restaurants or streets

- Purposive / judgmental sampling:- the researcher select participants based on specific criteria that are relevant to the study or it is a type of sampling in which a purpose is already there in the mind of the researcher & sample characteristics are pre-defined e.g. workers in the pencil factory.

- Quota sampling:- the researcher select participants based on certain quota that reflect the population characteristics such as gender or age groups.

- According to Clive seate: quota sampling is quicker and cheaper than simple random sampling.

- Snowball sampling:- it works on the referral principle. In which the research known only one respondent & other subjects are recommended by the first one & the process goes on just like the snowball. For e.g. survey of drug addicts, war widows etc.

Survey:

It is the quantitative research method used to collect data from a predefined group of respondents to gain information and insights on various topics of interest.

Surveys can be conducted in many ways like online surveys, telephones surveys, face to face, mail surveys etc.

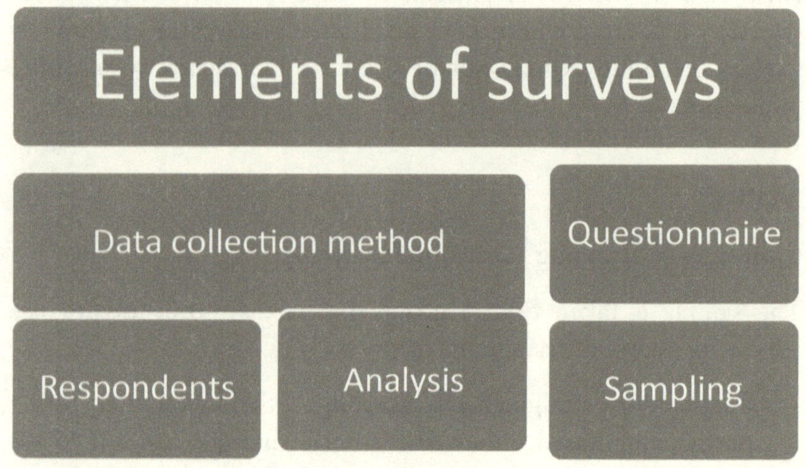

In surveys there are two types of questions.

Closed ended questions with MCQ.

Open ended questions they allows respondents to Answers in their own words.

Advantages of survey

- Easy to administer.

- Cost effective.

- Can be administered remotely.

- Close ended questions provide valuable data that can be quantified.

- Surveys collect a wide range of data from opinions to behaviour.

- Surveys can reach large populations quickly.

Disadvantages:

- Response rate is very low in online, email surveys.

- Respondents may be biased towards certain questions.

- It fails to gain the subjective experiences & opinions of respondents.

- In depth information can't be collected.

- Not possible for illiterate masses in online & email surveys.

- Research design:- it is the blue print or master plan to conduct research. It outlines the overall structure of the study & provide a framwork for making decision about what, how, when, where data will be collected.

Steps:

(1) Choice of topics.

(2) Collections of facts.

(3) Representation of facts.

(4) Hypothesis formulation.

(5) Testing & validation.

(6) Conclusion.

Types of research design:

(1) Exploratory research design:- to explore a concept which is unknown or no studies exist till now.

(2) Descriptive research design:- it is research to describe various events & social phenomenon & it is the most frequently used research design.

(3) Experimental research design:- it is used to done experimental studies i.e. laboratory experiments with one control groups & other variable group.

(4) PANEL research design:- or longitudinal research periodic information collected from a fixed panel or sample of respondents.

Hypothesis:- tentative statement about research topic which shows relations between two or more variables it is an untested statement which awaits validation.

According to stebbing:- every hypothesis springs from the union of knowledge & sagacity.

Sources of hypothesis:

(1) existing theoretical proposition. (2) Common sense (3) existing knowledge (4) research study (5) ancestral views & ideas (6) natural conditions.

Characteristic of a good hypothesis:

(1) The hypothesis should be clear & simple in language.

(2) It shouldn't be based on moral judgments, some facts should support the hypothesis.

(3) It should be specific & precise.

(4) Relevant to the study of research.

(5) It shows relation or inter connectedness Among variables.

(6) It should lead to theory building.

(7) Easy to validate it.

(8) Shows some generalization.

(9) Provide a framework for organizing and summarizing the results.

CHAPTER 6

CLASSICAL SOCIOLOGICAL THINKERS

AUGUSTE COMTE (1798-1857)

French philosopher.

Founding father of sociology & father of sociology.

His work laid the foundation of modern social science.

In his book positive philosophy-first- use the term sociology.

He believed in cerebral hygiene.

Main works of August comte:

(1) Positive philosophy in 6 vol.

(2) Positive polity in 4 vol.

(3) The prospectus of the scientific works required for the reorganization of society 1822

(4) Course of positive philosophy.

Contribution of Auguste comte:

Sociology as a science:- he coined the term sociology in 1838 & believed that it is the ultimate science this integrates all forms of human knowledge to study the society & its components.

He divided sociology into 2 parts

Social static,   social dynamic

Static part of the society i.e. structure of society studies social change & focus on social order.

Social Dynamic studies the changing Societal Patterns and issues.

In a brief:- definition of sociology by Auguste comte Sociology as the science of social phenomena subject to natural and invariable laws the discovery of which is the object of investigation

Laws of three stages:-

According to this concept the human societies and social change progress through 3 stages and he believed that last stage is the most advance stage in which humans have better control over science reasons logic and promotes progress.

- First stage:- theological stage /fictitious stage:

- Primitive societies:- believed in super natural forces

- Magic and religion dominates the mundane

Family is the basic unit:

Emotional bonds & strong attachment to family.

Worship natural forces:- polytheism dominance of priest and religious leaders.

Sub – stages within the theological stages

2ND STAGE:- metaphysical stage/abstract stage:- people become philosophical & believes in abstract reasoning and questions the supernatural and religious supremacy rise of philosophical thinking & ideas of natural law.

- Rise of legal society.

- Rise of collectivism & mutual respect.

- Enlightenment period –RUSSEAU , IMANUEL KANT AND MONTESQIEU

3rd stage:- positive stage/ scientific /advanced stage.

- Believes in scientific & experimental knowledge based on facts

- Rise of rationalism & develop scientific temper.

- Critical thinking and reasoning.

- Rise of industrial society

- Believes in humanity & universal order

- Love for the humanity.

Positivism:- according to comte positivism is a philosophy of science based on the idea that knowledge should be derived from scientific & empirical evidences rather then metaphysical or religious speculation.

According to comte:-positivism denotes any sociological approach which operates on the general assumption that the methods of physical science can be carried over in to the social science.

He devised the term in two ways.

(1) Positivism as a doctrine. (2) Positivism as a method.

(1) Positivism as a doctrine:-it envisaged that positivism is the only method to collect scientific, valid & reliable data & it should be used to study all social phenomena. He also believed that knowledge derived from sensory experiment which further bring social change & improve the social conditions in particular progress human condition.

(2) Positivism as a method:- positivism is a method or strategy to study social phenomenon

E.g. law of 3 stages.

(3) Religion of humanity.

Augusta comte developed the idea of a religion of humanity which means.

(1) secular & humanistic approach

(2) morality

(3) altruism

(4) humanity as the centre of everything

(5) religion without god

EMILE DURKHEIM (1858-1917)

French sociologist
Founding father of sociology

He was functionalist

Macro view of society & individual is subordinate to society

Society has a reality of its own over & above the individual who comprise it

He established the first ever department of sociology in Europe & was the first professor of sociology

According to him sociology is the science of social institutions

Society is sui-generis

Major works.

(1) Division of labour in society 1893

(2) Rules of sociological method 1895

(3) Suicide 1897.

(4) Elementary forms of religious life 1912

(5) Professional ethics and civic morAls

Contribution of EMILE DURKHEIM

Social facts:- he define social fact in his book. The rules of sociological method 1895.

He defined social fact as – social facts are ways of acting, thinking & feeling which are external to the individual & are endowed with the power of coercion by reason of which they control of him.

According to him the task of sociologist is to study social fact in a natural world which are external to the individual & exert force on him.

Social facts include laws, customs, moral belief, religions practices & language.

E.g. legal system.

Features of social facts.

(1) Externality:- exist outside the individual & must be seen apart from the individual.

(2) Constraining:-social fact exercise control over the individual.

(3) Generality:- these are general in nature & not to be confused the individual fact & interpretation & exist in the form of generalized perception.

(4) Independence:- social facts are independent of the will of individuals, individual can't change the social fact.

SUICIDE

Acc. To him suicide refers to every case of death resulting directly or indirectly from a positive or negative death performed by the victim himself & which strives to produce this result.

Suicide is caused due to social integration & regulation. On the basic of this he explained 4type of suicide.

(1) Egoistic suicide:- individual are not integrated into society & feel isolated i.e. low integration e.g. high suicide rate among childless and lonely persons.

(2) Altruistic suicide due to over integration individual into society who sacrifice their lives for the benefit of his country e.g. wars with enemy, soldiers.

(3) Anomic suicide:- results from a breakdown of social norms and a social regulation mostly due to economic depressions.

(4) Fatalistic suicide:- occurs when individuals feels excessively regulated and oppressed by societal norms or rules e.g. suicide by war prisoners or slaves.

DIVISION OF LABOUR

Division of labor: refers to differentiation, heterogeneity and complexity which hold the society together.

According to him dol is a social phenomenon & is product of autonomous development of society & dol is directly co-related with solidarity.

Solidarity

Organic	Mechanical
Simple dol	Complex dol
Primitive societies	Modern societies
Collectivism	Individualism
Repressive laws	Reformative laws
Informal relations	Formal relations

Mar Weber: 1864-1920

German sociologist; philosopher, legal scholar & political economist.

Founding father of sociology.

Weber is known for his rigorous analysis of how individuals motivations, cultural values and institutional structures shape society

Sociology is the science which attempts the interpretative understanding of social action in order thereby to arrive at a casual explanation of its course and effects

Major works:

(1) The protestant ethics and the sprits of capitalism

(2) The methodology of social sciences

(3) The sociology of religion.

(4) Economic & society.

(5) The city.

(6) The theory of social & economic organizations.

(7) From max Weber essays in sociology.

Contribution:

Ideal types:- an ideal types is an analytical construct that serves the investigator as a measuring rod to ascertain similarities as well as deviations in concrete cases. Ideal types is a type of objective methodology to study social Action these are derived from the real world but they are not the mirror image of the world Rather they are the one sided exaggerations of the essence of what goes on in the real world.

Types of ideal types:

(1) Ideal types of historical particular:- Study particular historical phenomena.

(2) Ideal types of abstract phenomena:- study abstract phenomena like social action & authority.

(3) Ideal types of particular behaviour:- e.g. political or economic behaviour.

(4) Structural ideas types:- these are forms taken by the causes & consequences of social action e.g. traditional authority & Rituals.

Social action:

An action is social by the virtue of the meaning attached to it by the actor, it takes into accounts the behavior of others and is hereby oriented it's course.

Types:

- Traditional:- based on traditional norms, customs & values. Exist in ancient societies.

- Instrumental Rational Action:- means & goals are rationally defined for e.g. invest in profit firms.

- Value- Rational Action:- on the basis of ethical values it is also known as wertrational e.g. charity.

- Affectual Action:- based on emotions & feelings. E.g. impulsive behavior during anger

AUTHORITY.

Authority:- is a form of legitimate power.

Types:

(1) Traditional authority:- based on customs traditions & inherited power. E.g. kings, Tribal chiefs.

(2) Charismatic authority:- based on the personal qualities and leadership of an individual e.g. charima of gandhiji

(3) Legal- Rational authority:- based on formal rules, laws and regulations e.g. Bureaucracy.

Bureaucracy:- is a type of hierarchal organization which is designed rationally to coordinate the work of many individuals in pursuit of large scale administrative tasks.

Features:

(1) Hierarchical structure:- Bureaucracy are organized into level with each level having clearly defined power.

(2) Specialization:- works are divided into specific roles with each individual performing specialized tasks

(3) Rules & regulations:- works within the Ambit of proper rules & regulations.

(4) Appointment based on eligibility criteria.

(5) Fixed salary allowance & pensions.

(6) Supervision of work by higher officials.

Religion:

According to Weber: religion is a belief in a supernatural power that is unable to be scientifically explained.

He believed religion is not just as a system of beliefs but a powerful social force that shapes individual behavior economic system & societal development.

Weber key works on religion.

(1) The protestant ethics & the spirit of capitalism (1905)

(2) The sociology of religion (1920)

(3) Studies on world religion i.e. Hinduism, Buddhism, Confucianism & Judaism.

KARL MARX (1818-1883)

German philosopher, economist, historian, sociologist & revolutionary socialist

He was critique of capitalism & promotes communism.

He laid the foundation of conflict perspective in sociology.

Major works:

(1) Des capital

(2) Holy family & the German ideology. (along with Engels)

(3) The economic manifesto of 1848.

Contribution:

(1) Historical materialism:- / materialistic interpretation of history.

The concept is defined in his book contribution to the critique of political economy 1859.

It is a method of interpreting history on the basic of material conditions that a changes over time.

There are two aspects of historical materialism

1 conception on the basic of economic infrastructure & social superstructure.

(2) Dialectical process which involves two opposing forces interact with each other & new structure are produced

i.e. thesis antithesis - synthesis.

Elements of historical materialism.

(1) Relations of production:- it involves relations at 2 levels in the process of capitalism

Relations between man & man

Relations depends on economic power with two classes bourgeoisie & proletariat.

Relation is subordinate i.e. proletariat are submissive bourgeoisie / haves

To upper classes. Subordinate & antagonistic relation proletariat haven't.

(2) Relation between, man & things:

Men are just the producer & maker have no control haves – control the owner ship rights

Over the production of goods.

Haven/ non ownership.

Force of production:- it includes tools, techniques equipment and skills required for production.

Mode of production:- Marx has conceptualized this society in term of 6stage or evolutionary mode of production.

(1) Primitive communism:- hunting gathering societies all are equal & had equal access to force of production.

Relation of production – based upon cooperation

(2) Ancient slave mode of production:

Masters – owners

Slaves subordinate relations with the masters.

(3) Feudalistic mode of production:

Feudal lords- land owner

Have

Antagonistic relations

With

Serfs/peasants

Forced to cultivate the land of feudal lords

(4) Capitalistic mode production:

o   Bourgeons- haves

o   Proletariat haven't

o   Antagonistic and subordinate relations between the two.

(5) Socialistic mode:- it is a mode in which proletariat will topple bourgeoisie & control force of production Marx calls it the dictatorship of proletariat.

(6) Advance communism:- it is utopian & final mode in which everyone had equal access to resources & no classes in the society at this dialectical principles ceases to stop

Class & class struggle:

Class:- refers to a group of people sharing the same position in the process of production.

Class struggle refers to the conflicting behaviour between the two classes means bourgeoisie & proletariat according to karl marx class struggle is the engine for the historical interpretation of history of mankind.

Class struggle takes the form of:

Economic exploitation	alienation revolution,
Bourgeosie exploit	alienation from
The lower class & create.	Self, society &
Surplus value.	Even from work potential

The actual revolution occurs with the transition of class in itself to class for itself

- Class in itself: classes are not aware of exploitation

- Class for itself: classes are aware of exploitation

As the class rises class consciousness chance of revolutionary potential increase & proletariat topple the upper class thus working class control the force of production and give rise to classless society.

Religion:- Marx called religion as the opium to the masses in his book a contribution to the critique of hegels philosophy of right (1843) religion is a drug which is used by the preacher to eases the pain and suppression caused by economy exploitation under capitalism.

Essential aspects of class struggle / class conflict:

- Rise of capitalism:- with the advent of capitalism divide between rich & poor increases and formation of two classes bourgeoisie and proletariat with this the importance of private property increases which further widen the inequality gap.

- Polarization of classes: In this process the rich get richer and the poor get poorer there are intermediate classes like small capitalist and petty bourgeoisie & lumpen proletariat which falls under the category of proletariat RAYMOND MURRAY calls this process as proletarinisation

- Theory of surplus value:- increasing profits of capitalist leads to exploitation & submissions of labor class capitalist use this surplus value to enhance productivity.

Profit to increase their base which further drenched labor into a vicious cycle of inequality & exploitation

- Pauperization:- in the words of Marx the wealth of the rich is swelled by by a large profits with corresponding increase in mass poverty, slavery and exploitation of proletariat

- Alienation:- labor feels alienated from production process and relations of production.

- Class solidity & antagonism:- it occurs when class is itself converts into class for itself.

- Revolution & the rise of proletariat:- when the alienation reaches its peak the class consciousness develops among lower class which give rise to a revolution. & Topple the upper class.

- Formation of communist society:- it is the final STAGe in which each and everyone has equal share and leads to the formation of classless and casteless societies

CHAPTER 7

INDIAN SOCIOLOGICAL THOUGHT

Ideological / textual perspective: the literary meanings of indology means Study of Indian society and culture on basis of traditions, religions, ancient legal and historical texts for e.g. Ramayana, Mahabharata, Vedas, Upanishads, historical monuments , paintings & rock addicts follower of indology G.S GHURYE Louis Dumont. Radhakamal Mukherjee IRAWATI KARWE.

G.S GHURYE (1893-1984)
Brahmin:
Father of modern indology/ Indian sociology
Trained Sanskrit scholar

Influenced by western scholar like WHR rivers founded the Indian sociological society and journal sociological bulletin

MENTORED M.N Shrinivas, AR Desai, MSA Rao IRAWATI KARVE, IP Desai
PhD under AC hidden on cost and race in India
principle architect of the Dept of sociology in Bombay

held survey ON sex habit of middle class people in Bombay (1930).

Promote theoretical pluralism i.e. multiple ideas and theories/ perspectives can coexist and be applied to understand complex phenomena.

Major work

(1) Cast and race in India

(2) Culture and society

(3) Religious consciousness

(4) WhITHER India

(5) Social tension in India

(6) Family & kin in indo European culture

Contributions

Cast system:- he devised the concept of cast system in his book caste and race in India according to him cast orginates from gangetic plains & spread to other area via diffusion and caste is a endogamous and closed kin network

Features of caste

Segmental division … horizontally divided

In Hindus Rajput Bhagat chamars are horizontally divided

Hierarchy:

brahmins-top class / superior

Kshatriyas

….Vaishyas

Shudras/untouchables /depressed caste

Pollution & purity:- higher caste are pure in nature and lower cast are termed as polluted & highest caste maintaining distance from lower ones.

Civil & a religious disabilities & privileges of different sections

Higher caste - privileges in social hierarchy temple entry

Lover cast-> barred from temples and forced to live outskirts of cities in a polluted and dilapidated areas.

Lake of choice of occupation.

Restriction on marriage -> practised endogamy

gotra endogamy: not marry in the same gotra

Marriage between persons of same gotra is incest taboo

Spinda exogamy i.e. prohibiled degree of kin 5 from maternal side

7 from paternal side. Social order based on dharmashastra.

Indian sadhus wrote briefly on religion and consider religion as dynamic as Indian society.

In his book Indian sadhus. A sadhu is supposed to be detached from all caste norms & social scenario but in Indian society sadhus played an important role in maintaining the social order and acts as a link between common man and God.

Culture:- according to Ghurye culture is the central element for understanding society and its evolutions and culture is defined as the entire heritage of mankind.

He devised 5 foundational values of culture

(1) Religious consciousness

(2) Conscience

(3) Justice

(4) Free pursuit of knowledge & free expression

(5) Toleration

Village & tribes:

According to him village as the centre of Indian society and deeply interacted with the city life though village are self - sufficient but they engage with outside in all aspects of life.

He called tribes as backward Hindus and differentiated them as hinduised tribes partially hinduised tribes & hill section according to him their backwardness was due to their imperfect integration into Hindu society.

Ghurye is criticised for over Hinduised view of Indian society and his Studies mostly based on textual documents and studies cannot be guaranteed & validated.

Structural Functional perspective:

It is a sociological theory that views society as a complex system whose parts work together to promote stability and harmony i.e. independence of societal components such as institutional norms and roles that function to maintain social order and cohesion

Promoters of structural functionalism.

M.N Srinivas

S.C Dube

Mckim Marriot

M.N SRINIVAS (1916-1999)

Mysore, Brahmin Family'

Intensive study of coorgs with different castes like Brahmins, kaniyas, panikas

Society can be studied from two perspectives one is field view and other is book view

M.N srinivas is the proponent of field view

Major works:

(1) Marriage & family in Mysore 1942

(2) Indian villages

(3) Caste in modern india & other essays 1962

(4) The remembered village.

Dominant cast & other essays:

Contribution of M.N srinivas

Sanskritization:- the term Sanskritization was coined by MN Srinivas and he defined it as the process by which low caste or tribe or other groups takes over the customs, rituals beliefs, ideology and style of life of a high and in particular a twice born.

Book religion and society among the coorgs of south India.

Simply Sanskritization is the process by which low caste people tries to imitate the life style of higher caste mostly Brahmins.

Features:

- Imitation of upper caste lifestyle.

- Imitate the dress speech cultural practices

- Abandon non veg, iquor & alcohol follow proper sanitation going to temples and performing brahminic rituals and practices

- Social mobility:- it is an important ladder of upward social mobility to exchange their social status in the society hierarchy.

Religious and social change

Performing brahmim festivals like Diwali, Holi, navratri & brings attitudinal changes among low caste imposed cultural dominance: it signifies Brahmin culture as superior and acts as the yardsticks of behaviour in a society.

Criticism:

(1) De - sanskritization in Punjab & jats in Haryana

(2) It only brings in social status not social condition

(3) Limited avenues of structural mobility & social mobility

(4) imposes superiority of brahmins on other and neglect of non Hindu traditions.

Westernization:- M.N Srinivas defines westernization as the changes brought about in India society & cultural as a result of over 150 years of British rule it means follow western practices it is only a cultural change & not show any structural change.

According to Srivinas there are 3 levels of westernization.

(1) Primary westernization:- minority Indians come in contacts with the western people.

(2) Secondary westernization:- masses comes in contact with the primary beneficiaries of westernization.

(3) Tertiary westernization:- large masses come in direct contract with western cultural traits & changes in dress, food, style, habits etc

Features / aspects of westernization.

(1) Cultural:- change in food habits i.e. dominos, pizza, burger, western short dresses.

   Marriage practices, live in relationship, Genz culture, individualism, cinema, fashion, travelling.

(2) Education:- modern universities scientific research methods innovation, skills, training, critical thinking At.

(3) Social norms & values: promotes secularism gender equalities, human rights, civil liberties, free speech, border free.etc

(4) Political & legal system: rule of law, human rights framwork, global organization like UN, unesco, property rights, right to forgotten and reformative laws.

(5) Economic system: promotes import & export,, globalization, liberalization, privatization.

(6) Communication:- rise of mass media social media press, journals, newspaper, pamphlets.

Social mobility:- breaking the notions of crossing the seas upward mobility promotes social order & stability brings harmony & progress rise of brotherhood.

Dominant caste:- M.N Srinivas studied village Rampura in Mysore coined the term dominant caste he defined dominant caste in terms of 6 features.

1.   Sizeable amount of agricultural land.

2.   Numerical strength / strength of numbers

3.   High place in the local hierarchy

4.   Western education

5.   Jobs in administration

6.   Urban source of income e.g. in Rampur village the peasants are at the bottom of hierarch but they posses lands and numerically have political influence over village affairs

M N srinives views on caste:-

1.   Hierarchy

2.   Occupational differentiation.

3.   Restriction on commensality, dress, speech, and customs

4.   Concepts of pure & impure caste.

5.   Caste panchayats and assemblies

6.   Segmentary on the basic of endogamy, common occupation, common culture and common authority.

Marxist / conflict perspective:- it is a sociological perspective which understand society in terms of a process of historical developments in dialectical materialism terms.

Proponent of Marxism:

- D P Mukherjee

- A R desai

- Ramakrishna mukherjee.

D P MUKHERJEE (1894-1961)

One of the founding fathers of sociology in India

west Bengal middle class families

He was knows as marxiologist i.e. social scientist of Marxism

He used dialectical interpretation to study Indian traditions and cultural transformation.

Major works

- Diversities

- Basic concepts in sociology

- Personality &the social sciences

- Problems of Indian youth.

- Introduction to music

Contribution:

1. Personality:- D P admits that Indian social life is like the life of bees and beavers and the Indians are almost regimented people but the beauty of it is that the majority of us don't feel regimented

2. Modernization: is a process of expansion, elevation, revitalization of traditional values and cultural patterns. According to D P modernisation should be studied in terms of dialectical relation from traditions.

Tradition:

According to D P tradition comes from the root trader which means to transmit.

Dialectics of tradition & modernity:

- Tradition:- refers to long established customs, beliefs, practices & social norms that are passed down through generations.

- Modernity:- refers to social & culture changes characterized by new ways of thinking, regionalism, scientific advancement industrialization and the rise of individualism

Dialectical new:

Mukherjee claimed that tradition & modernity are not opposite but co- exist & re- in force each other in a dialectical interpretation. He presumed that Indian society's modernization should not reject tradition wholly solly but instead reinterpret & adapt it to contemporary needs.

Assumptions:

(1) Synthesis of tradition & modernity:- it means modernity doesn't means modern values & western lifestyle but Indians modernity is shaped by traditional norms & values.

(2) Dynamic tradition:- traditions are dynamic in nature & transforms without changing their true essence.

Cultural integrity:- it promotes cultural integrity of traditional & modern values & somehow it leads to neglect of traditional values.

Class & social structure:- dynamism from tradition to modernity leads to rise of new classes & changes in the social structure & hierarchy.

Imtiyaz Ahmed:- Indian sociologist: Studies issue related to caste, communalism & the sociology of religion.

Major works:

(1) Cast & social stratification among Muslims in India (1973)

(2) Secularism & its critics. 1998.

Contributions:

Communalism & secularism:

He argued that communal tensions in India expectedly between Hindus & Muslims is continuously escalating.

Communalism is only due to vested political interest. Rather then genuine religious conflicts he also advocated for secularism as a vital principle for maintaining social harmony in Indias pluralistic society.

Ashrafization & ajlafization:- the concept of Ashrafization and ajlafization coined by the imtiyaz ahmed in his book. Caste & social stratification among Muslims in India. These concept are integral to the understanding of Islamic elements in Indian society.

Ashrafization:- & ajlafization is similar to sanskritization of MN srinivas. The term Ashrafization drives from the word ashraf which refers to Muslim of superior lineage i.e. sayyids, sheikhs, mughals, & pathans it is a sociological term that refers to the process by which lower cast / non elite Muslims groups in south Asia (India) tries to imitate the cultural social and religious practices of the upper caste Ashrafs.

Caste hierarchy:

- Ashrafs – sayyids, sheikhs, mughal, pathans/educated elite and superior class

- Ajlaf – converted from hindus artisanal labourer/weavers, butchers carpenters barbers

- Azral – untouchables, dalits scavengers/converted from low caste hindus

- Ajlafization is also similar to Ashrafization in which low caste untouchables & converted tries to imitate the practices of Ajlafs.

CHAPTER 8

SOCIAL CHANGE

Social change is define as the changes in the culture, behaviour, social institution & structures overtime or we can say changes that occurred in the desired direction is called social change.

According to GIDDINS - social change refers to alteration in basic structures of a social group or society.

Features of social change:

(1) Universal process:- found in all & every societies.

(2) Continuity it is a continuous process.

(3) Various from of social change i.e. political, cultural, behavioral etc.

(4) Social change is irregular & relative.

(5) Not predictable:- it is difficult to know the exact level of social changes because social change is subjective in nature & occurred over a period of time.

It is a smooth & gradual process.

Causes / aspects of social change:

(1) Modernization adopting modern values.

(2) Westernization, industrialization, sanskritization, Ashrafization.

(3) Constitution & laws.

(4) Education

(5) International organization i.e. UN, UNESCO, world bank

(6) Urbanization

(7) Social moments like LGBTQIA

Theories of social change:

(1) Linear theories / evolutionary model

(2) Cyclical theory

(3) Structural functionalist theory

(4) Conflict theory

Linear theory of social change:- according to linear theory societies changes from simple to complex. It is based on theories of biological evolution or Darwin's fittest theory" survival of fittest.

Linear theory is also known by the name of evolutionary model & changes occurred in a unidirectional way.

(1) August comte:- devised the concept of law of 3 stages in which social changes occurred in stages from theological TO meta physical TO positivistic / rational the last stage is the most advance stage based on critical thinking & logical reasoning.

(2) Spencer organismic analogy:- he is known as social Darwinist as his idea were influenced by biological theory of evolution. According to Spencer social change involves differentiation of simple things into complex. On this basIs the process of evolution takes place in a manner like simple- compound – doubly compound

Trebly compound

Or

Militant societies   ->

industrial societies

Agricultural societies

modern / rational

Collectivism

individualism

Simple division of labor

complex division of labor

(3) E.B Taylor:- social change followed the linear path in a manner like

Animism monotheism	polytheism
Worship INANIMATE things worship single god	many gods like
PREVALENT in tribal & hunting like CHRISTIANS and muslims Societies	Hindus societies

(4) Ferdinand tonnies:- German sociologist used the concept of Gemeinschaft & gesselschaft to donate the linear social changes.

Gemeinschaft	> gesselschaft
Primitive society	socials rational will
Community contractual &	heterogeneity
Natural will & sacred	formal relations specialized
Traditions	& complex division of labor
Homogenous group	
Religion dominants	
Informal relations	

(5) Robert Redfield:- changes occurred in a linear fashion from folk to urban

Folk	> urban
Homogenous & primitive	rational & heterogenous society
Agricultural societies	urban economy
Rural economy	

Cyclic theories /cyclic model:- according to this model social change occurs in a cyclical process i.e. rise, growth, decline-renewal. These theories refute the evolutionary models.

The main proponents:-

1. OSWALD SPENGLER:- in his book "decline of the west mentioned destruction of civilization. He studies 8 major civilizations of the world including the west. He Said THAT modern society is at Last stage i.e. old age and further concluded that all western societies are at the verge of decay.

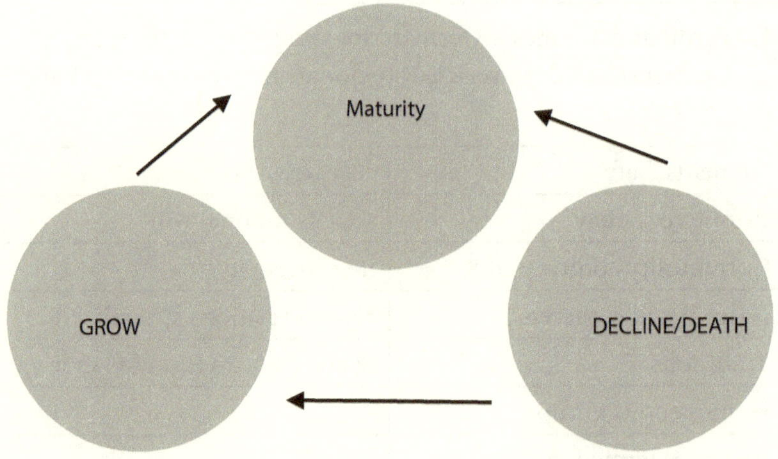

2. Vilfred pareto:- in book TREATIES ON GENERAL SOCIOLOGY devised the theory of circulation of elites.

The major proposition is that social change occurs through the circulations of elites periodically replaced by new elites.

RULLING MINORITY / Lions-foxes

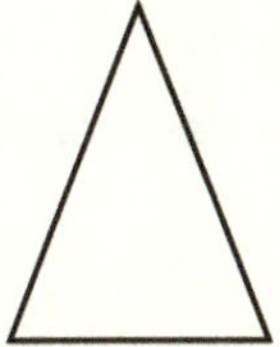

Ruled masses /MAJORITY POPULATION

PRITIM SOROKIN:- in his book social & cultural dynamics 1938 derived a cyclical model to explain the process of social change.

The main idea is that societies oscillate between different cultural and intellectual orientations i.e. idealogical and sensate,

Social change IS like a swinging pendulum between ideation &

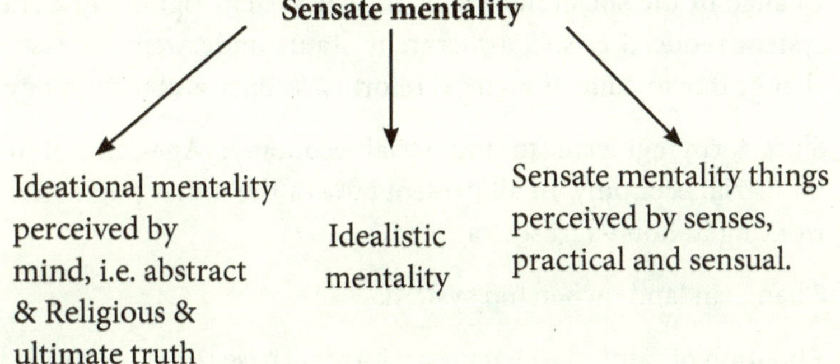

Conflict model of social change:- according to this model social change in the societies occur due to conflict between different groups within society which are unequal in power resources & interests key elements of conflict model are.

(1) Power inequality among different classes i.e. wide gulf between rich and poor.

(2) Class struggle: different class in the society fight for power due to unequal distribution of resources.

(3) Social change through revolution: conflict theorist like Marx argues that social change is often revolutionary rather than evolutionary

(4) Revolution occurs when class consciousness arises.

Main proponent:

Karl Marx bourgeoisie / haves

Conflict between the two

Class give rise to social change proletariat / haven't

Structural & functional changes in rural society:

Structural changes.

(1) Change in the social hierarchy & caste system rigidity of caste system reduced & social hierarchy status underwent a drastic change due to education, legal reforms, science and technology.

(2) Shift form agrarian to industrial economy: Agricultural to industrial economy. In all present 60% of the indias population working in non –agri sector

(3) Change in land ownership system:

Abolition of zamindari tenancy reforms. These reforms changed the ownership pattern & surplus land transferred to the lower & detrenched classes

(4) Shift from joint family to nuclear family

(5) Participation of women in the workforce

(6) Migration & urbanization

(7) Decentralization of power & governance through panchayati raj institution Road connectivity & diversification of trade

Functional changes in rural society.

1. political participation & awareness: rural areas are involved in election process due to increasing awareness

2. **changing social norms:**

    o **Late marriage** is not taboo

    o **Choose** partner is a right

    o **Divergence** towards small family size

    o **Changing** religious ideology

3. Rising rural entrepreneurship with the help of banks and microfinance institutions

4. Increasing awareness regarding health and hygiene Menstrual health, postmortem stress

5. Gender Stereotypes changed

6. women are equal

7. property rights and

8. right to remarry, divorce options

9. Commercialization of agriculture

STRUCTURAL AND FUNCTIONAL CHARGES IN URBAN SOCIETY

Structural Changes:

1. Rise of new classes and formation of class based hierarchies i.e. Engineers, Doctors/scientists supervisors staff

2. Expanding middle class

3. Nuclear family increasing due to increasing modernization and westernization

4. Rise of informal sector

5. Political decentralization through municipality act

6. Formation of megacities

7. Increasing ruler influx and density

8. Crowding and congestion

9. GENZ culture Yolo culture

10. Rise of single parent household

11. Concept of sologamy/nogamy

12. Rise of oldage homes, silver dividend

FUNCTIONAL CHANGES

1. Economic diversification service based

2. knowledge based economies

3. Role reversal women's participation in the work force increased

4. Formal and contractual social relationship

5. Rise of new urban movements like metoo movement, and clean water and air movement

6. Concept of smart city, historical towns and cities

7.   Changes in the lifestyle and life chances

8.   Urban planning

9.   Environmental sustainability, urban inequality

10.   Rise of NGO's for animals and humanity

Social order: deviance and conformity

Social order is defined as the structured and organized set of relationship institution and norms that helped in maintaining order and stability in society thereby maintaining its equilibrium. It is essential to maintain balance among various institution for the smooth functioning of society and to maintain peace security and cooperation among member of society.

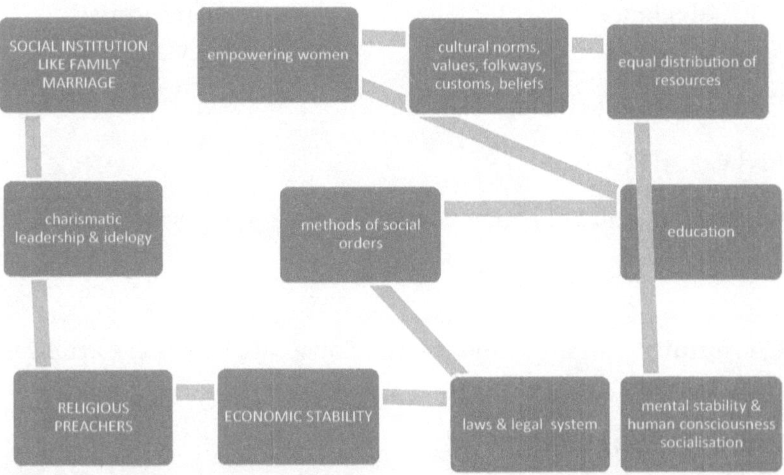

Approaches to social order:

(1) **Functionalist approach**: According to this approach society is like a motor car composed of various integrating and interdependent parts which together promote order and stability. E.g: there are various important institution in the society which helps in promoting order like family education, religion.

      o   Family promotes values and brings socialization.

- o Education equality, unity, excellence, healthy competition

- o Religion peace, brotherhood .

- o Talcot parson devised a AGIL scheme to maintain order.

- o The main proponents are TALCOT PARSONS, EMILE DURKHEIM believes in values consensus

(2) conflict perspective:- social order is maintain through power and domination with Some groups at the expense of other & others are submissive and subordinate to the rulling group and elites karl marx theory of class struggle circulation of elites theory by vilfred pareto .

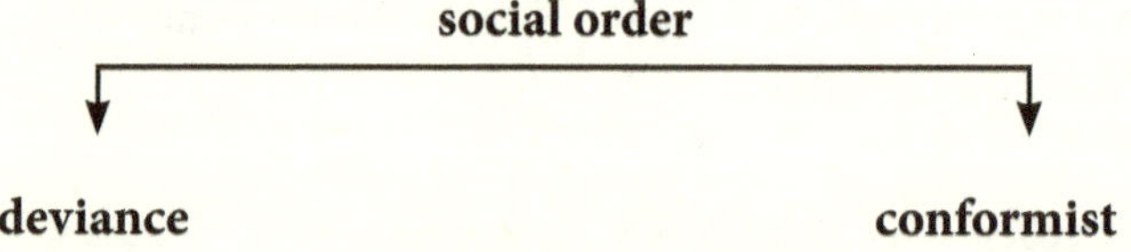

Don't conform to the institutionalized

ENDS AND GOALS

follow rules and regulation & conformed to the norms & VALUES OF SOCIETY

Conformity:- means actions of individuals are based on established rules & expectations of the society at large.

Reason for conformity:

(1) Socialization:- people are properly & keenly socialized from a young age to follow social norms & values.

(2) Hierarchy in society:- people always follow their ancestors & parents.

(3) Fear of sanctions or rewards & punishment.

Rewards – respect, medals moral boost

Punishment – fine, imprisonment, social disapproval

Ideology:- ideology and mental stability of individuals also leads to conformity of norms

RELIGIOUS:- concept of hell and heaven in every religions helps to make individual humane & genuine

Deviance:- the concept of deviance was given by Robert Merton in his book social structure and anomie 1938. It is an analysis of relationship between culture, structure and anomie Merton theory of deviance is based on his own conception of anomie which was drawn in the backdrop of the "the great economic recession.

According to Merton: deviance is defined as a situation in which there is a rift between culturally defined goals & means to achieve them, on the basis of anomie conditions he defined several types of deviant behaviour.

(1) Conformist:- one who follow both goals & means e.g. school students.

(2) Innovator:- one who follow culturally defined goals but rejects socially defined means e.g. scientist thiefs and robbers.

(3) Ritualist:- one who accepts the socially defined means but fails to get the goals e.g. bureaucrats.

(4) Retreatist:- it involves the rejection of both means & goals e.g. alcoholics, drug addicts.

Rebellion:- it involves the rejection of both goals & means at first & then the creation of new means & goals revolutionaries.

TYPES	MEANS	GOALS	EXAMPLE
+++++Conformist	+	+	School students
Innovator	-	+	Scientists, thieves
Ritualist	+	-	Bureaucrats
Retreatist	-	-	Drug addicts
Rebellion	- ▶ +	- ▶ +	Revolutionaries

CHAPTER 9

SOCIAL STRUCTURE AND PROCESSES IN INDIAN SOCIETY

Social structure:- organized pattern of relationship, roles, institution & systems within a society that shape how individual & groups interact. It is the master plan or yardstick for society how to influence & shape the behavior of individuals and maintain order & stability in the society. It operates at two levels.

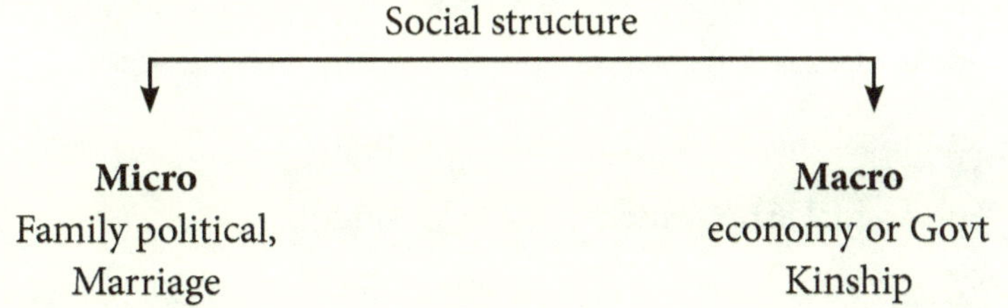

Social structure is the organized set of social institution their influence on individual & their roles & shaping the individuals & societies.

Components of social structure:

(1) Status:- position of individual in a society

Ascribed   achieved

By birth   though education & skill efforts

(2) Role: expected behavior, responsibilities and obligations linked to a particular status.

(3) INSTITUTION:

Family – socialization, emotional support.

Education – skill, knowledge, values.

Economy – productions, distributions & consumption.

Govt – rules, regulations, policies.

Religion – moral guidance, cohesion & brotherhood.

(4) Groups: groups of two or more people who share a similar sense of identity.

1 group – small, informed groups (family)

2 group – work oriented formal groups (job)

In group – in side close group – own village

Out groups – out side 2 group – other village

Reference group – influence group

(5) Social classes & networks.   Ultra rich classes.

Stratification   upper

Hierarchial arrangement   middle

Lower

Social norms, folkways, mores, laws.

SOCIAL PROCESSES

Refer to the manner in which various social group & individual interact with each other in society or simply it is defined as social relationship that exists among people.

Various processes are:

(1) Cooperation

(2) Competition

(3) Conflict

(4) Accommodation

(5) Assimilation

(6) Acculturation

(7) Socialization

(8) Segregation

(9) Integration

(10) Amalgamation [melting pot]

(11) Diffusion and division of labour

Nature / Feature of social process:

1. Universal:- social process are present in all human societies regardless of time &location

2. Regulated by norms and values

3. Methods of social change.

4. Agents of order & stability

5. work at both micro ¯o levels.

6. Regulated by social hierarchy & societal norms

7. mutual & Reciprocals relation.

8. interrelated and interdependent

9. continuous & dynamic in Nature

TYPES

1. **Cooperation:** it is the process in which individuals, group's organization, NGO'S work together to achieve common goals. It is the most basic and important social process in societies.

   Team work in sports activities, joint project, collective efforts for community improvement.

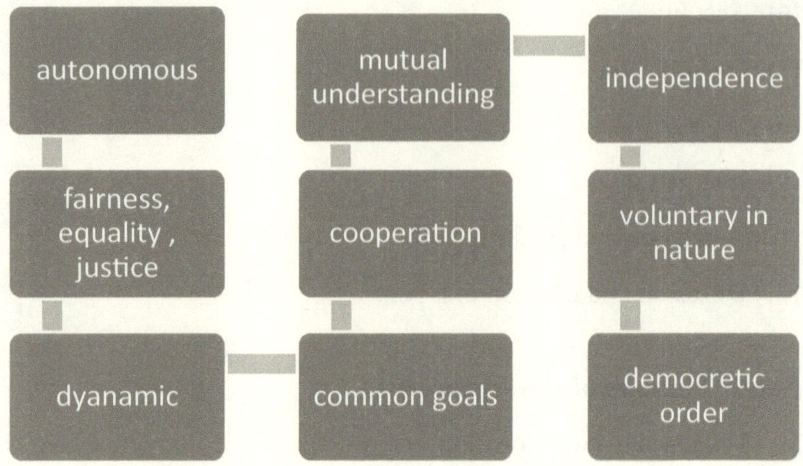

2. **Competition:-** it the opposite of cooperation. It is based on Darwin theory of survival of existence.

It is defined as the struggle between individual group or organization for resources, power, status, recognition & authority.

It motivates individuals to improve their performance, faster economic growth & promote technological advancement.

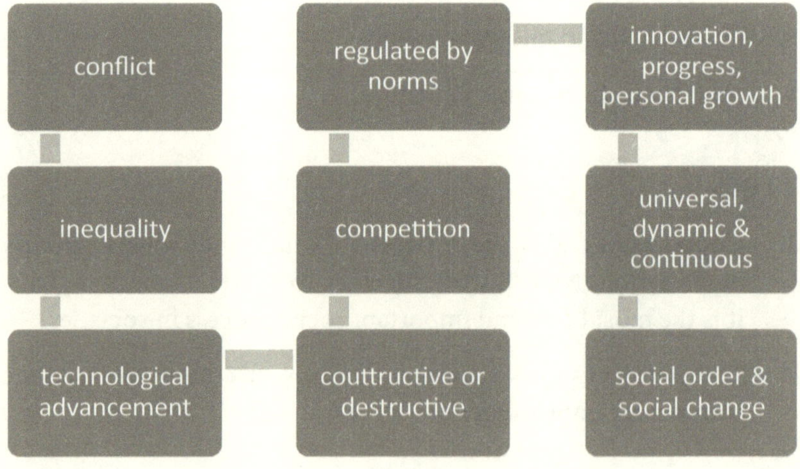

Accommodation:- it is a process in which individuals or groups tries to compromise or adjust with other groups simply it is adjustment of individuals in a different hostile group

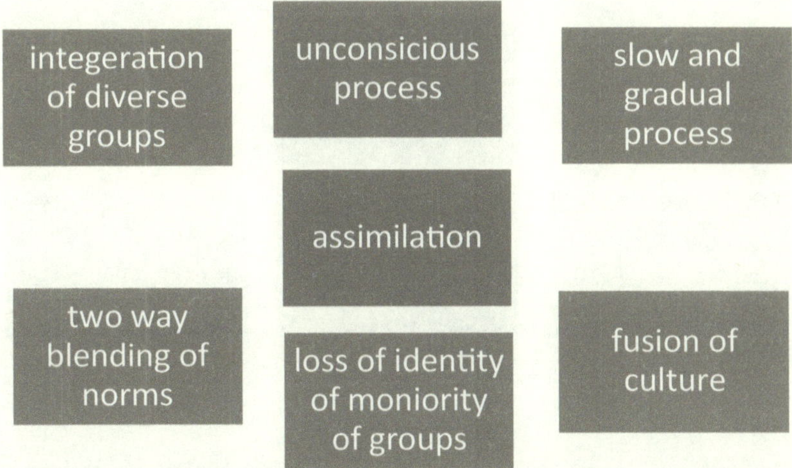

Acculturation:- it is the process by which individuals or groups from different culture comes into contact and exchange cultural elements

i.e. norms values folkways , food packages, language dilactics without complete assimilation into large groups

Amalgamation:- (melting point)

It is the process in which two different groups comes together to form a new culture or society. e.g. Immigrant from various continents forms USA.

Dol/ division of labour:- is the process, in which works are divided among groups & individuals on the basisof age, gender, specialization & efficiency.

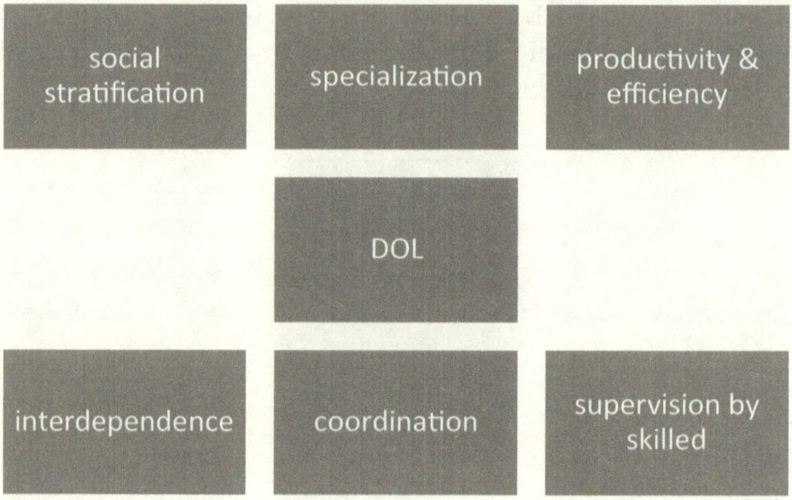

social stratification

specialization

productivity & efficiency

DOL

interdependence

coordination

supervision by skilled

CHAPTER 10

MISCELLANEOUS

ECOLOGY

The term ecology first coined by German biologist –Ernst Haekel

It is a Greek word oikos meaning home or place to live in & logos meaning study.

Thus ecology is the scientific study of the relationship between living organisms & their physical environment.

Environment:- The place where we live or everything that surround or affect an organism during it life time is collectively known as environment.

The environment is not static but composed of biotic & abiotic factors.

Environment

Biotic	a biotic
Animals'	sunlight
Humans'	energy
Symbionts	temperatures
Decomposers	insulation
Saprophytes	gravity
Parasites	soil
Green plant	topography
Non green plants	fire
	Water
	Radiation
	Heat flow

Levels of organization in ecology:-

Individuals	Basic unit-body of organs, organelles or other parts that join to carry out various process of life.
Population	Group of organisms of same species.
Community Major and Minor	Population of different species forms community
Ecosystem	Structural &functional unit of biosphere composed of biotic and abiotic factors.
Biome	Large geographical area characterized by its climate vegetation and animal's life.
Biosphere	Sum of all ecosystem including all living organisms and the environment in which they live.

Relationship between ecology social environment

The relationship between ecology & social environment is a complex interplay between natural ecosystem & human society. The various aspects of inte-relationship are

(1) **Interdependence**

- o Both human and environment are entirely interdependent on each other example mutual coexistence all the important and critical resources for survival are gathered from environment

- o For e.g.: ecosystem provides food fodder and essential l services like clean air water purification and pollination process that support human health & well being

(2) **Environmental impact**

- o ->increasing urbanization put a pressure on land and increase the threshold limits of ecosystem

- o Deforestation and loss of habitat

- o changes in land use pattern

- o pollution –water, air, land, sky

(3) **Environmental uses**

- Sustainability of ecosystem for healthy living
- Increasing men –animal conflict
- Decreasing water table
- Increasing Global warming, melting of polar ice caps and glacier

(4) **Impact of climate change**

Rise of natural disasters –floods droughts, landslides

- Social disruptions
- Changing weather patterns
- Threat of pandemic like covid 19

(5) **Conservation**

- Govt political
- Afforestation
- life campaign
- judicious utilization of resources
- rainwater harvesting
- environmental education & awareness

OBJECTIVITY

Is an approach in which the attitude of an investigator is detached unprejudiced value free & free from biases.

Acc. To Robert Bierstadt: Objectivity means the conclusion arrived at as result of inquiry & investigation are independent of the race, color, creed, occupation, nationality, religion, moral preference & political predisposition of the investigator.

Objectivity can be achieved by avoiding things in the process of research as under:

1. **choice of topic:** personal preferences avoided

2. **collection of facts:** objectivity in facts and observation

3. **interpretation of fact**: personal opinion and ideas avoided

4. **formation of theory:** based on hypothesis

5. **testing:** use of scientific methods approval of validity and reliability.

CULTURAL LAG

The concept was given by W.F ogburn. It is a process in which material cultures changes at a greater pace than non-material cultures

Science and technology and social change

- Discovery of fertility drugs

- Artificial insemination, invitro fertilization, genetic engineering, cloning

- Internet, mass media, face book, computer robotic

- Artificial intelligence

- Specialization of skills and mechanization of agriculture

- Rise of electric vehicles

- Thus science and technology accompany us from cradle to grave

Relationship between sociology and common science.

Though there are differences in nature and subject matter of sociology and common science but in reality both reinforce each other it can be clearly explained with the help of diagram as under.

COMMON SENSE PROVIDES RAW DATA FOR RESEARCH HYPOTHESIS ....SOCIOLOGY CORRECTS STEREOTYPES AND ENRICHES

SOCIO CONCEPTS AND VOCABULARY

BIBLIOGRAPHY

1. *seema, Nitin Sangwan essential sociology.*

2. *Surjit sen Gupta – introductory sociology.*

3. *N J Smelser – sociology - an introduction*

4. *A R Redcliffe Brown – structure and Function in Primitive society.*

5. *Kingsley Davis – Human Society.*

6. *Lewis A Loser - Masters of sociological thought.*

7. *Maciver and Page – "society introduction analysis"*

8. *Bottommore, T.B – "Sociology"- A Guide to problems and literature.*

9. *Shanker Rao, C.N Sociology Vol.I & Vol. II*

10. *William J. Goode – The Family*

11. *Robert Bierstedt - The social order.*

12. *Ream Ahuja – social Problems inn India.*

13. *Harlambos M. & Heveld R.M – Sociology – Themes and perspectives.*

14. *B.K. Nagia – Indiann Sociological though.*

OTHER SOURCES

1. *Oxford dictionary of sociology.*

2.   *Collins dictionary of sociology.*

3.   *The new encyclopaedia Britannica*

4.   *India Year book 2023.*

5.   *Newspaper Analysis.*

Basic Questions for all exams.

1.   *Do you think women empowerment in India is backstabbing the gender equality.*

2.   *Why marriage system in India undergoes adverse changes.*

3.   *How one as a student & parent brings equality in society.*

4.   *Why there is rising gender violence.*

5.   *What all the basic reasons for the exploitation of women in India.*

6.   *Why Gender equality is utmost to achieve 100% literacy role in India.*

7.   *Why domestic engineers/mothers suffers from malnutrition.*

8.   *Explain the reason for growing militancy in J&k are lacking in social and political parameters.*

9.   *Why people of j and k are lacking in social and political paremeters.*

10.   *Why the students of J&K are not excelling in top competitive exams.*

11.   *Do you think Govt. is giving much importance to J & k after the aboragation of Article 370.*

12.   *Do you abrogation of article 370 is a master stock for the center.*

13.   *Laws in Indian Judiciary is women oriented.*

THE END

* 9 7 9 8 8 9 6 9 9 7 3 7 5 *